The JUDGE MULLIGAN POISONING *and Other* HISTORIC LEXINGTON CRIMES

KEVEN MCQUEEN

Published by The History Press
An imprint of Arcadia Publishing
Charleston, SC
www.historypress.com

First published 2025

Manufactured in the United States

ISBN 9781467159371

Library of Congress Control Number: 2025935716

Dedicated to Philo T. Farnsworth,

because I don't think anyone has ever dedicated anything to him.

CONTENTS

ACKNOWLEDGEMENTS

A gracious and low-sweeping bow goes to:

Eastern Kentucky University Department of English; Eastern Kentucky University Interlibrary Loan Department; Amy Hawkins McQueen and Quentin Hawkins; Evan Holbrook; Denise and Amber Hughes; Darrell and Swecia McQueen; Darren, Alison, Elizabeth Renee and Charles David McQueen; Kyle McQueen; Michael, Lori and Blaine McQueen; Craig and Debbie Smith; Mia Temple; and Joe Gartrell, Ashley Hill and everyone at The History Press. Also, the Expediter of all things.

Friend me on Facebook—as George MacDonald almost said, "A true Facebook friend is forever a friend." And find my propaganda at www.KevenMcQueenStories.com.

1
OVERKILL

In the mid-1840s, Alexander T. Hays (or Hayes) was the proprietor of a Lexington drugstore. He was well-regarded but thought to be a simpleton, even a harmless lunatic, which makes one wonder why anyone would patronize a pharmacy run by a man who might be foolish or crazy. But I digress. The point is that on the morning of October 17, 1846, Hays's body was found on Nicholasville Road, at what was then the outskirts of town.

Whoever wanted Hays dead didn't believe in subtlety or leaving things to chance. The city was horrified by the level of overkill. Hays had a huge gash under his right ear and a mangled right hand and had been disemboweled. These injuries seemed to have been inflicted with a Bowie knife. There was no blood at the scene, so the body had likely been hauled to the spot on a wagon and dumped. Hair clutched in the dead man's right hand was the only evidence. Today, investigators would rejoice at such an opportunity to get the attacker's DNA, but in 1846, it wasn't much of a clue.

In addition to the Bowie knife, the killer used a smaller blade to stab Hays fifteen times in the chest. The *Lexington Observer and Reporter* opined that the victim "was, perhaps, more horribly cut up, mangled and mutilated than any man ever was before." In fact, the druggist was more badly butchered than initial reports related. Further scrutiny by the coroner revealed that Hays had been stabbed *eighty-six* separate times and shot in the head. "There was not a vital part about him that was not most shockingly perforated," said the *Observer and Reporter*. Of this multiplicity of wounds, twenty would have been fatal.

The mayor held a public meeting on October 18 to figure out how best to investigate. The city council suggested a $250 reward (equivalent to slightly over $6,600 in modern currency). In November, the amount was upped to $500 (currently $13,200). The advertisement that offered the bounty promised it would be paid to anyone who provided a tip that collared the killer. So desperate were authorities to catch the murderer that even the tipster's race didn't matter: "[I]t shall be paid to anyone, *White or Black.*"

On October 23, investigators disinterred Hays's pathetic remains so they could examine his wounds again, all eighty-six of them. Exactly what they were hoping to discover, they did not inform the press. The inquest jury's verdict, released a month later, told only too clearly how the probe was faring: "[A]fter a patient and laborious investigation, running through upwards of three weeks, they were unable to elicit evidence on which they could convict any individual."

"[I]t will be utterly impossible for the author of this most cruel and inhuman outrage to escape," the *Observer and Reporter* had predicted back on October 21 with ill-founded optimism. Hays's killer was never captured—but it is possible that he struck in Lexington at least once more.

On October 31, 1847, slightly more than a year after the Hays murder, an elderly widowed grocer named Elizabeth Warren was found murdered. Her killer had rifled her purse, emptied the till and set the building ablaze. The fire was quickly extinguished, and murder was evident. As it did in Hays's case, the city offered a $500 reward for information. But like the earlier case, the money was never collected.

An unnamed man living in Cincinnati's Eighth Ward was arrested on suspicion of murder on November 8. He was taken to Lexington and questioned. The city marshal was convinced of his innocence and released him. That was the end of the story forever—at least on this plane of existence.

2

MORE ON THE HAZARDS OF SHOPKEEPING

Shopkeepers of the mid-nineteenth century were often targets of crime. The more isolated their business establishments, the more likely they were to suffer violence from wandering brigands. Another Lexington example unfolded soon after the murders of Alexander Hays and Elizabeth Warren.

Native German Henry Yellman kept a country store on Tates Creek Road, then about ten miles from the city. He lived alone in his storeroom. On the night of December 10, 1848, two men chopped at Yellman's head with a hatchet and stole his savings, the existence of which was not exactly a neighborhood secret. A customer found his body the next morning.

The recent Hays and Warren crimes were invoked during the investigation. In April 1849, the *Louisville Courier* remarked, "[F]or a time it was feared that the murderers, like those who murdered Hays and the old woman in Lexington, might escape detection."

In January 1849, two enslaved men named Henry and Aaron were arrested. The few sources that detail the crime do not mention the grounds for suspicion. Perhaps it was merely their proximity to the crime scene, as their enslavers Richard and Lewis Martin lived near Yellman's store. At first, each blamed the other.

Then Aaron voluntarily confessed, saying he was the sole killer. He pleaded guilty twice more, once to one of the Martins and again to the editor of the *Lexington Atlas*. On both occasions, he implicated Henry as an accomplice. They had planned the crime for months, he said.

Henry and Aaron were tried on April 12 and hanged six weeks later, on June 1. The *Lexington Reporter and Observer* summarized: "They made a full confession of the crime before trial, and repeated it again under the gallows, as we understand, acknowledging the justice of their punishment and resign[ed] to the merited fate they had brought upon themselves."

Did Henry and Aaron also kill Hays and Warren? Maybe. But they were so penitent at the end that if they were guilty of additional crimes, they probably would have confessed to those, too.

3

MURDER AMONG THE SWEETS, OR: JEALOUS MUCH?

On the Yuletide evening of December 29, 1853, Mrs. Weigart entered G.H. Dahlinghaus's candy store in Lexington. The clerk, Luther Cushing, described as "a very orderly, respectable young man," must have been in a sugary mood—perhaps it was the influence of his surroundings—as he patted the potential customer on the back and said something she found highly offensive. "I'll tell my husband!" she cried.

Before the narrative proceeds, no doubt the reader wonders what Cushing said that was such an insult. I will tell you, but you must have smelling salts or a living will handy, just in case you can't handle it.

Cushing had said, "What will you have, pretty?" Well, maybe it was the *way* he said it.

Anyhow, the clerk apologized profusely after making this faux pas, protesting that he had mistaken her for someone else. Perhaps that was true, but Mrs. Weigart was having none of it. She charged out of the store and told her hot-tempered husband, William. Overcome with jealousy, he stomped into the confectionery about forty-five minutes after Cushing's grave offense.

Cushing must have been worried in the interim, as he borrowed a gun from a friend should self-defense be necessary. It didn't do him any good. As soon as William Weigart entered, he fired a revolver four times at the fleeing clerk. The first three shots missed, but the fourth killed Cushing as he crouched behind the counter among all those sweets. Both men made a fatal mistake that day: Cushing flirted with a married lady, and Weigart lost his temper and shot a man in a helpless position—in the back, at that. Cushing fired once into the floor as he ran, perhaps as a warning shot. There was no way Weigart could claim self-defense under such circumstances.

Both Weigarts were arrested. On New Year's Day 1854, William was remanded to jail while his wife was set free. Cushing was buried by his friends from the Independent Order of Odd Fellows.

The temperamental husband went on trial on June 14. He was found guilty the next day, after the jury deliberated only a few minutes. His attorneys applied to Judge Goodloe for a retrial. Denied! Perhaps as a caution to other jealous husbands who might feel inclined to shoot up candy store clerks, on June 24, Goodloe gave the prisoner the harshest punishment allowed by the law.

"Do you have anything to say why the sentence of death should not be pronounced against you?"

"No," replied a subdued Weigart.

After urging Weigart to get right with God, Goodloe pronounced August 12 as his date for hanging.

Usually, an execution was delayed several times as a condemned man's attorneys made appeal after appeal. Not in this case. On the morning of August 12, Weigart stood on the gallows in Lexington and became, as Ophelia said of Hamlet, "the observed of all observers." He calmly stated that he expected to find peace in the afterlife. As the evil moment drew ever nearer, Weigart seemed to want to get it all over with. Rather than wait for the trapdoor to open, he jumped off the platform after the rope was adjusted around his neck, before the two reverends who accompanied him had a chance to pray and before he made the final oration every crowd who attended a hanging fully expected. Arguably, he died by suicide rather than execution.

Weigart was "the first White person executed in Fayette County during the present century," said a newspaper, which also noted that his passing was "long and painful." There is no record of what happened to his widow, but hopefully, she learned how to take a compliment.

4

FRAZER'S HOMECOMING SURPRISE

The crime "almost transcends belief, it is of so horrible nature." So said a reporter about a murder that occurred near Lexington in 1854.

The events were set in motion when farmer James O. Frazer (also called Fraser and Frazier in contemporary accounts—take your pick) went to New York to sell livestock. He was gone four months. On September 30, he informed his family by telegraph that he would be home that night. His neighbor and business partner Lewis Castleman picked him up at the train depot and gave him a ride home. Then Castleman returned to his own house.

About half an hour later, Castleman heard gunfire reverberating from the Frazer homestead. He hurried over. All the lights were out, and the residents took their sweet time before they finally opened the door. Castleman found his neighbor on a couch, dead from a shotgun blast. Mrs. Elizabeth Frazer and her eleven-year-old daughter were upstairs, and twenty-three-year-old George Grigg (also called Griggs and Gregg), the overseer, was downstairs.

"What happened here?" asked Castleman.

"He shot himself by accident," Grigg explained. "He was trying to kill a rat." He had just gotten home after a grueling four-month trip, you see, and immediately had the yen to shoot rats.

Something about the situation—perhaps the inappropriate demeanor of the house's occupants or the absurd rat-killing story—didn't ring true to Castleman. Then again, his bovine excrement detector might have been set off because the victim of the so-called accidental self-shooting was badly bruised, had three broken ribs, sported *two* gunshot wounds (one bullet went through his hand, stomach and liver, and the other went through his head) and had a slashed throat. Then there was the fact that the damp carpet had been taken up and washed *very recently*. Also, Grigg, the overseer, whom Castleman had seen earlier that evening when he dropped Frazer off at his house, was wearing different clothes than those he was wearing previously. Grigg said that he had helped his wounded employer to the floor, gotten bloodstained and thought it was a good idea to change clothes—so he wouldn't look suspicious, one presumes. He must have changed in quite a hurry, as he popped the buttons off his pants. Those items were found on the floor by the kitchen fireplace, yet he couldn't produce the bloody clothes. He never did, nor could he say where they went.

Castleman thought it fishy, too, that when Mrs. Frazer entered the room containing the gory corpse of her husband, she seemed indifferent to the circumstance. Indeed, she behaved as though such a thing were an everyday occurrence and nothing to get excited about. Her version of events was hardly more believable than Grigg's. She concurred that her husband had shot himself accidentally just minutes after coming home, because he just *had* to celebrate his homecoming by killing that rodent. His body was on the couch because she had asked Grigg to place it there. Since Grigg was a "man of all work," wasn't moving a bloody gunshot victim part of his job? Meanwhile, as Grigg was manipulating the corpse and changing his own clothes, Mrs. Frazer thought it an opportune time to wash the carpet. (Domestic chores won't do themselves!) They performed all these activities in a locked house with the lights out.

It is evident that Grigg and Mrs. Frazer did not have time to hatch a better story. Castleman alerted the police; under the circumstances, what else could he do? Neighbors had long suspected an affair between the overseer and Mrs. Frazer, and uncharitable persons opined that one or both had conspired to remove the farmer from the picture so their happiness might be complete. Mr. Grigg and Mrs. Frazer were arrested.

Investigators noted the suspicious facts right away, and the coroner's inquest on October 2 uncovered another. The version of events as told by Grigg, Mrs. Frazer and her daughter matched in every trivial detail, leading police to believe they had rehearsed a fixed story. A man who attended the inquest heard the three speak and said that their stories dovetailed so perfectly, it sounded as though they were reading off the same handbill.

Some mysteries remained. The examination of the body was performed with such carelessness that the press complained about it. In particular, the marks on Mr. Frazer's throat, which seemed evidence of throttling, were not scientifically scrutinized. Doctors' opinions differed about the nature of the rib fractures, but all of this seems beside the point, unless someone wanted to argue that the farmer had broken his own ribs when he fell. The big question concerned not his ribs but his gunshot wounds. The bullet that went through his hand and tore off a thumb before penetrating his entrails suggests a defensive wound that occurred when Frazer instinctively held up his hand.

One of Mrs. Frazer's partisans said that she was "a member of one of the oldest and most respectable families in the state," and was "characterized among her acquaintances by the gentleness of her disposition." As for Grigg, he previously had never shown anything but good character. Their attorney, Roger Hanson, gave what was deemed "one of the ablest speeches ever delivered in the courtroom." But their influence, reputation and top-flight lawyer were not enough to sway the jury. They had to stand trial for murder and were held at a $5,000 bond each, an astronomical sum at the time, which suggests no one was willing to risk letting them walk free.

The trial began in mid-February 1855. The jury visited the Frazer farmhouse on February 18 and spent the following two days hearing speeches by Shy and Beck (for the prosecution) and Hanson, Johnson and Robinson (the defense). The jury retired on February 21. Surprisingly, considering the evidence against Grigg and Mrs. Frazer, the jury was hung, with seven for acquittal and five for conviction.

Their second trial started on June 21. This time around, the jury was composed entirely of Bourbon Countians. If the prosecution believed they could not get a fair trial from Lexingtonians but could win a conviction with an imported jury, they were in for a profound shock. On June 23, the prisoners were acquitted. It was said that the members believed the well-rehearsed story the victim's young daughter told on the witness stand rather than the physical evidence.

Many in Lexington thought Mrs. Frazer and Grigg got away with Mr. Frazer's murder—a very ham-fisted, unsubtle, poorly planned murder. "Public opinion settled down upon the conviction of their guilt," remarked a *Louisville Journal* editorial years later. No doubt, many persons muttered adages such as "what goes around, comes around" and "as you sow, so shall you reap." If they did this, their dark wishes for revenge came true.

Not long after the verdict, the Frazer daughter's dress caught fire, and she burned to death. The suspicious whispered that it was no accident, that she had been "put out of the way" before her conscience started persecuting her.

Mrs. Frazer sold the farm and took up with Grigg, which lends credence to the rumors about their relationship. They moved to Mason County, probably to escape the staring eye and the wagging tongue. In April 1857, news broke that a mob had entered Mr. and Mrs. Grigg's house and used a knife to remove a portion of Mr. Grigg's anatomy that he undoubtedly regretted to lose—and which likely got him into so much trouble in the first place.

5

DARWINIAN STRUGGLE FOR LIFE

At 8:00 p.m. on February 15, 1858, Darwin Payne stuck a knife into fellow Lexingtonian John F. White, aka "Boss," who died instantly. Payne insisted it was done in self-defense. That's all the information the earliest news reports provided. The event took on a sleazier air as more facts emerged. Payne didn't stab White once but several times, and with a fearsomely large Bowie knife, the fatal wound reaching from the throat to the sternum. Both assailant and victim were drunk. They had just left a "coffeehouse," a genteel, yet sarcastic, euphemism for a saloon.

The grand jury found a true bill of murder against Payne, who still pleaded self-defense. A reporter using the pseudonym "The Corporal" described him as "quite a young man, and very respectably connected." The writer spent several more lines grandiloquently describing the grief of Payne's widowed mother, who had a "heart broken and bruised with sorrow," and noting that "a sympathizing heart is a spring of pure water bursting forth from the mountainside" and much more then-fashionable mushiness.

Payne's trial was scheduled to begin on August 14. On the same day, four men, including one named McChesney, enticed a German bartender named George Henry, who happened to work at that so-called Mulberry Street coffeehouse and was scheduled to appear as a witness against Payne, to have a nice piping hot bowl of soup—their treat! He declined, but after the men left, he unwisely ate the soup and, soon afterward, was the sickest German bartender Lexington had seen in a while. The suspicious timing made some wonder if Payne's supporters were trying to eliminate a witness.

A doctor who examined the ejected contents of the barkeep's stomach found no traces of mineral poison. The German recovered, so it appears he wasn't poisoned after all and that his sudden illness after consuming the soup was just a coincidence. Considering that it was summertime in the days before easy refrigeration, it is reasonable to believe that he may have suffered a case of food poisoning. Still, one can't help but wonder why these strangers offered Henry a free bowl of soup in the first place and why they were so darned insistent about it.

After the usual delays, the murder trial began on August 24. Darwin Payne was convicted and sentenced to four years in prison. But luck was with him. The court of appeals reversed the decision in January 1859, the same year that another Darwin published *On the Origin of Species*. Someone wasn't convinced, as Payne again went on trial for killing White on July 25, which would seem to be a violation of the Constitutional double jeopardy clause that forbids a second prosecution for the same crime. As late as June 1860, the circuit court in Woodford County—there was a change in venue from Fayette County—was trying Payne for the same old murder. The jury was hung, and there seems to be no record of a fourth trial. Payne was young, free and the perfect age to change his name and be drafted into the Civil War, which, for all we know, was exactly what happened to him, since he disappears from historical view.

6

LEXINGTON LYNCHING

Very early on July 10, 1858, a fine Lexington summer morning, William Barker was occupied at the Water Street market house, trying to whittle on John McChesney. Could he have been the same McChesney who was accused of poisoning the German bartender who witnessed Darwin Payne's stabbing of John White a month later? As for Barker, he had a reputation for carrying concealed weapons. City Marshal Joseph Beard, who had been on the job for less than a year, came to make an arrest. Barker stabbed him in the heart with a Bowie knife that was huge—even by Bowie knife standards—leaving a wound four inches wide. Marshal Beard gasped twice and was no more.

Brave persons disarmed and arrested Barker and dragged him off to jail. Soon after word of the marshal's death in the line of duty got out, the jail was surrounded by citizens who were impatient to see justice carried out—surely, it would have been in the natural course of things, as Barker had no reasonable excuse for his actions. The citizens were joined by toughs who just wondered what it would be like to stretch a neck. Someone rang the courthouse bell; others rang the city's fire alarm bells. A chant sliced the humid air: "Hang him! Hang him!" A man gave the affair a pseudo-parliamentary flavor by shouting, "All in favor of hanging Barker, say, 'Aye!'" The hundred or so "jurors" gave their verdict as one: "*Aye!* Hang him!" James O. Harrison and Roger W. Hanson tried to calm everyone down, but this mob had initiative.

The impromptu court confronted the jailer, saying, "Give us the key, or we'll take it." The jailer didn't have the spirit to argue with this flagrant "either/or" logical fallacy, and before Barker knew it, he was standing on the courthouse lawn. There was no ready-built gallows and no trees fit for the task at hand, but never underestimate a highly motivated mob's creativity. Masked men shoved Barker into the courthouse. Someone slid a pole through a second-story window, fastened one end of a rope to it and tied the other end around Barker's neck.

"Pray!" clamored the crowd, which didn't want it said of them that they would send a man to hell before giving him a chance to avoid that destination.

"I have nothing to pray for," answered Barker, refusing the generous offer. "You can hang me and be [bloodcurdling blasphemy deleted]."

Barker was pushed out the window. The rope broke, and the fall knocked him unconscious. A second rope was found, and the cop killer was left dangling for an hour and a half so that all might view him and learn a lesson. By 8:00 a.m., the mob had dispersed, the city was quiet and all was back to normal—if one discounted that grotesque corpse swinging from the courthouse window.

If it was any consolation to Marshal Beard's spirit, his funeral was the largest and most ornate seen in Lexington since Henry Clay's.

7

HANGING SOME DUMMIES, OR: THE TREE STOOGES

Mr. Lafayette Shelby entered Swift and Robbins's store in Lexington and shot clerk Henry Horine through the head. The date was January 10, 1846, and the reason for this argument and its abrupt ending do not appear. Allegedly, both were intoxicated, so that might be reason enough.

Shelby went on trial on July 1. He was no gutter trash; he was the grandson of Kentucky's first governor, Isaac Shelby, and his family was so prominent that one of his courtroom defenders was none other than the Great Compromiser himself, Henry Clay. The case went to the jury on July 4. They could reach no agreement after several days' confinement and were discharged. Shelby was bailed out and walked the streets as free as you please.

But certain elements of the public were *not* pleased by Shelby being turned loose or by the hung jury, so they did a little hanging of their own—a hanging of effigies, that is, which is nicer than lynching the genuine article but also gets the point across. When the insects droned and the hazy summer sun rose on July 13, Lexingtonians beheld dummies swinging from a tree in front of the courthouse, symbolizing Judge Richard Buckner and the eight jurymen who had held out for an acquittal. Evidently, Henry Clay was too respected to be singled out for such vicarious vengeance. The eight jurors were G. Clugston, J.M. Kidd, P.E. Todhunter, William Bowman, William Curd, James Penny, Samuel Downing and James Devers. So, if you are a descendant of any of these gentlemen, congratulations! You can boast that your ancestor was hanged in effigy. And how I, for one, envy you.

A generic effigy hanging. Imagine eight more effigies, and you can grasp the extravagance of the Lexington dummy lynching. *Public domain.*

The description of the figures suggests that the mob had absorbed the too-obvious, unsubtle symbolism found in editorial cartoons then and now. The judge's dummy had a mask and a hollow head, symbolizing his perceived *brainlessness*—get it? The dummy had one hand rested on a pocket, on which was inscribed "bribery." The effigy also bore the inscription "A judge without justice." The substitutes for the eight jury members were each decorated with the word "Perjury." One included the additional insult "Money gets me." The courthouse janitor tried to remove the dummies before citizens saw them, but taking down just one involved some work, let alone nine. Besides, court officials refused to allow it, saying, "We had no hand in putting them there, and we will have none in taking them away." So, the nine insults swung away in the breeze for the better part of the morning, there to stay until the vandals had a change of heart and retrieved them.

To make matters worse, Captain Robert Wilson opened a second-story courthouse window (Could it have been the same window from which William Barker was lynched, as mentioned in the last story?) and delivered a rabble-rousing oration. He pointed out that if the situation had been reversed and Horine had killed Shelby, he would have been convicted and hanged within two days. But *no*! Lafayette Shelby was a wealthy *aristocrat* and could blow out the brains of anyone he took a notion to, "and this perjured jury has let the murderer go out unwhipped of justice." Then he proposed that the mob "burn in the streets the infamous jurors." (To clarify, he meant the dummies, not the humans.) He also recommended that citizens demand the resignation of Judge Buckner. Captain Wilson, who was running for public office, asserted that "on his election…it would be the proudest act of his life to present that resolution to Judge Buckner." Everything the captain proposed was greeted with whoops and approving catcalls.

The crowd appointed a committee to cut down the effigies, which was done to stirring martial music. A procession mounted the dummies on poles—a sight that would have warmed the heart of Vlad the Impaler—and carried them away as the band played "The Rogue's March," a mocking piece of military music that was traditionally played when humiliated soldiers were drummed out of the service. Then, surely enough, they tossed the figures in a heap on Cheapside and burned them to ashes. The entire drama could have been avoided if the courthouse officials had simply let the janitor dispose of the dummies as quickly as possible. A newspaper correspondent who signed his letter "Spectator" (And he certainly had a lot to spectate that day!) wrote in despair, "What is the state of the public mind when such things happen in broad daylight?…May heaven save us from the whirlpools of anarchy."

To Lexington's credit, folks calmed down quickly after this cathartic exercise. But one juror, Todhunter, was so unpopular that he was burned in effigy twice more, in Nicholasville and Liberty. The *Lexington Observer and Reporter*, on July 22, published a long letter signed by many citizens who commended the much-abused Judge Buckner. When the *Louisville Courier* reprinted the encomium, it filled a column and a half of tiny type on a very large sheet.

At the end of September 1846, Judge Buckner was given notice of an intended impeachment pushed by a relative of the victim, Horine. Shelby's

Henry Clay, who was too well-esteemed in Lexington to be hanged in effigy. *Public domain.*

second trial was scheduled for October, and some thought the timing was no coincidence, since if the judge were successfully forced to resign, it would reflect badly on Shelby. Henry Clay, still interested in the case, argued for a continuance. Using the effigy hanging and Captain Wilson's speech as illustrations, he expressed concern that an impartial jury could not be established. Clay may have been correct; an anti-Buckner Lexington correspondent told the *Louisville Courier*, in a letter published on October 9, "Public opinion regards [Shelby] as a murderer in the first degree. That opinion has never abated—never will abate." Clay won the day, and Shelby's trial was delayed until March 1847. Ironically, the temper tantrum the mob threw back in July resulted in a further postponement of justice. Judge Buckner was not impeached, so the hotheads failed at that, too.

Shelby's trial was put off again until April 1848. The court spent March 31 trying and failing to find an impartial jury. By April 7, only 4 members had been accepted by both the prosecution and defense; by April 18, only 9 had been accepted. Time was running out. If the trial was not held within a week, the case could not be tried in the present term. By April 26, only 11 out of 1,600 potential jurors had passed muster, and the defense still hadn't used any of its 12 possible peremptory challenges.

Shelby was not tried a second time. He moved to Texas. There are two contrasting versions of his later years. One says that he was himself murdered near Dexter, Missouri, in 1859. The other maintains that he was seen in Lexington only once more on a brief visit during the Civil War. No one bothered him. He wasn't even hanged and burned in effigy.

8

A STUDY IN CALMNESS

The press deemed it "one of the most ghastly and sickening murders that has happened in Lexington in its history." It occurred where it might have been least expected, in the center of town in the home of John Woolfolk, the head of "one of the wealthiest and best families in the city." The victim was the family's maid, Betty Shea, aged twenty-two and originally from Carlisle. She was described as having "a handsome figure, with fine, wavy hair, [and] attractive features." (A very unflattering likeness of her appears in the *Courier-Journal* from June 25, 1889, followed by a more reasonable one in the February 28, 1890 issue.)

At 7:00 a.m. on Monday, April 1, 1889, the Woolfolks' cook knocked on the door to Shea's quarters. Receiving no answer, she entered and saw the maid dead on the floor with up to fifteen blows to the head, a long cut on top of her crushed skull and her face covered with a shawl. The police were notified and arrived within minutes. The blood had not yet congealed, and the body was still warm. A modern FBI profiler might have inferred that since Shea's face was covered, her killer was not a stranger but a guilt-wracked individual who had close ties to her. The furniture in her room was in disarray, indicating a struggle. There had been a violent storm the night before, which must have masked the sounds of battle; also, the maid's quarters were located some distance from the main part of the house. However, detectives thought the room looked more ransacked than haphazardly wrecked, as though Betty's killer had been searching for something.

A mighty unflattering likeness of Betty Shea from the *Louisville Courier-Journal*, June 25, 1889. *Courtesy of the* Louisville Courier-Journal.

Inquiries to the family indicated that Betty had a character beyond reproach. Pieces soon fell easily into place. With whom had Shea been spending time lately? Twenty-six-year-old Thomas O'Brien, a disreputable character who had been arrested a year before for killing Henry Metcalfe and acquitted on grounds of self-defense. He also had been charged with stealing a gold watch in 1886. The Woolfolks' coachman had often carried notes from the maid to O'Brien. The night just before her murder, Betty had told the cook that she and O'Brien would soon be married.

O'Brien, the likeliest suspect, was arrested just three hours after the discovery of the corpse. "Sure, I spent some time with Betty last night," he said. "But I didn't have nothing to do with no murder!" Conversely, he told *Lexington Leader* reporter C.C. Gribben that he had *not* been in Betty's room Sunday night. His telling two diametrically opposed stories soon after his arrest was not promising. Certain townsfolk muttered lynching threats—also not an encouraging sign. As an interesting comment on human nature, the Irish immigrant population of Lexington had always stood by O'Brien and defended his antisocial antics, but now that he was accused of killing "one of their own," they abandoned him like so many leprechauns fleeing a teetotalers' convention.

On April 3, Betty was buried in her family plot in the Catholic Cemetery in Paris, Kentucky. The next day, investigators made intriguing discoveries. For one thing, although Betty had confided her impending marriage to the cook, she and Thomas had already secretly married under assumed names in Cincinnati the previous September. Then there was a letter from Tom to Betty, which had been found in her dress pocket, promising to visit her on the night that turned out to be her last. Additionally, a pair of pants known to be O'Brien's were found bloodstained with $160 sewn up inside them. Betty had been frugal with her wages, and it appeared O'Brien had stolen his secret wife's savings. In the room of sex worker Lizzie Adams, O'Brien's *other* girlfriend whom he called "Baby Mine," police found a bloody pair of leaden knuckles wrapped in a towel and hidden in a bureau drawer. The knuckles were applied to the wounds on Betty's head before her burial and fit perfectly. Adams was arrested on suspicion of being an accomplice, perhaps even the mastermind.

O'Brien's trial was held on April 5 before a packed audience. The lynching talk had not lessened, and the size of the crowd made officials jumpy. They sneaked O'Shea into the courtroom through the back door. Thus began O'Brien's nonchalance in the shadow of the noose, a source of amazement to the press and public in the months ahead. The only indifferent being in the room was the prisoner himself. At one point, he even enjoyed a good cigar.

One of the most significant witnesses was O'Brien's pal Frank Reynolds, to whom the prisoner had once said that he had "gotten a girl in a delicate condition" but vowed he would not marry her. Despite O'Brien's determined assertion not to marry Betty, he had done so because she was pregnant. Afterward, he decided that he liked another woman better, perhaps Lizzie. Not only that, but he was also presently engaged to Mattie Laughlin of Richland, Indiana, and was scheduled to marry her in May. He had not bothered to divorce Betty before pledging his troth to Mattie, so pregnant Betty's death was very convenient for his wedding plans. He "desired to desecrate other hearthstones," as a reporter said, which meant that O'Brien intended to ruin other happy homes.

A jailer testified that he had overheard O'Brien telling his brother that he had something hidden in Lizzie Adams's room, and he asked if he would please retrieve it. Lizzie Moberly, the owner of the house where Adams dwelt, testified that she had found the leaden knuckles in her room and notified the police.

Because some important witnesses had not been found, the case was delayed until June 16. Again, the courtroom drew enormous crowds, and O'Brien kept up his mask of studied unconcern. One telling piece of evidence was a letter he had written to Lizzie Adams, in which he quaintly said he'd "bet his life to a ginger cake" that he would be acquitted. But he also made a veiled reference to what sounded like the murder of Betty Shea: "If you had known everything before, it could not have changed the result. I could not have changed it; no earthly power could have changed it. It was horrible, but unavoidable, so far as I was concerned." Neither O'Brien nor any of his defenders seemed quite willing to volunteer what "it" referred to.

Betty Shea. Now that's more like it! *Louisville Courier-Journal*, February 28, 1890. *Courtesy of the* Louisville Courier-Journal.

Left: Tom O'Brien. *Louisville Courier-Journal*, March 3, 1888. *Courtesy of the* Louisville Courier-Journal.

Right: Sheriff James Rogers, who was tasked with hanging O'Brien. *Louisville Courier-Journal*, February 28, 1890. *Courtesy of the* Louisville Courier-Journal.

And then came a witness the defense was not expecting, who "fell on [them] like a thunderclap." A Black girl, Kate White, testified that she had encountered O'Brien and Shea having a vociferous argument in the street a few hours before the murder. White recounted that the argument had gone something like this:

> *Shea: Why didn't you keep that promise you made?* [Other testimony indicated that she had been angered because O'Brien refused to make their secret marriage public, which, of course he couldn't do, since he planned to marry another woman in a matter of weeks. Likely, this was the promise Betty meant.]
> *O'Brien: I've promised lots of things I've never done!*

Later, White happened to see O'Brien, and he demanded to know if she had overheard the argument. (Nothing suspicious about that!)

During closing arguments on June 21, jurors were noticeably in tears during the defense's summation—but they were weeping for Shea and her

The scaffold awaits. *Louisville Courier-Journal*, February 28, 1890. *Courtesy of the* Louisville Courier-Journal.

family, not O'Brien. This may have augured the verdict, which came on June 22. That evening, when the decision was anticipated, the courtroom was crammed with humanity, more than ever before—to say nothing of the additional one thousand people outside. One witness said people filled the halls, rotunda, transoms and even the windows. One man who tried to exit this Black Hole of Lexington found himself in such a tight squeeze that his coat and vest buttons were torn off. The defendant was calm as ever, but he was noticeably pale. The teeming masses were not disappointed, though O'Brien surely was, even if he didn't show it. The verdict was guilty, with a recommendation of the death penalty. O'Brien reacted by lighting up a cigar. He lost his cool only when he heard shouts issuing from outside. But he relaxed when he was told it was not a lynch mob; rather, it was merely a throng of people happy to hear that he would be hanged, which was much better. It came out later that the crowd outside had every intention of stringing up O'Brien if he had not been found guilty.

The record does not provide the reaction of O'Brien's fiancée, the badly deceived Mattie Laughlin of Richland, Indiana.

Two days later, Judge Morton set the hanging for August 24. O'Brien remained supernaturally calm. His counsel made a motion for a new trial. They were far more agitated than he. On December 5, 1889, the court of appeals upheld the original verdict. The prisoner took the news with his usual composure. At least the delay bought him about six months' worth of life.

His alleged accomplice, Lizzie Adams, drops from the headlines, so she was evidently never charged.

At noon on February 27, 1890, after having a good night's sleep and a refreshing oatmeal breakfast, O'Brien trudged up an all-too-short flight of stairs in the Lexington Prison. Everyone wondered if he would he maintain his eerie calm to the end. He did, even proclaiming, "This is the happiest day of my life." The hangman helped make O'Brien's happy day even more joyful. Betty Shea's brothers were in attendance, and the proceedings gladdened them as well. But O'Brien's family was not so pleased.

9

THE HARRIS-MERRITT SOAP OPERA

The only close-up eyewitness to the events in Lexington's Gratz Park—the only witness who was not directly involved in the drama, at least—was Professor J.P. Nelson, who heard two gunshots that summer night and a man shouting, "I have caught the — — — — at last!" Contemporary papers don't relate exactly what the man said, but as the censored phrase contained four words, it is easy to fill in the blanks—literally. Then a man came running up a path, pursued by another brandishing a gun. Professor Nelson prudently stepped out of their way. The man in the back fired two shots at the man in the lead. The first shot wounded the man, while the second was fatal. The professor hastily found pressing business elsewhere, but he was followed by the assassin, who asked in censorable speech, "Have you seen anything of that —— woman?" Nelson answered in the negative, and the man ran away.

Police arrested the slayer without incident. He was Jacob F. Harris, a thirty-four-year-old "drummer" (traveling salesman, so called in those days because they drummed up trade) who had a sneaking suspicion that his wife, Effie, age twenty-four, was cheating on him. She had been working for two months as a copyist to Thomas H. Merritt, a pension lawyer. Harris trusted his wife implicitly until his sister-in-law Gussie Thompson told him that Effie had been going on buggy rides with her boss lately. On this evening, July 9, 1897, Harris saw Merritt strolling down Short Street and thought he would play detective. He followed Merritt into Gratz Park, hid and, for nearly an hour, watched Merritt and Effie sitting together. Harris nearly lost his mind on the spot when he saw Effie sitting in Merritt's lap, hugging and kissing him. He burst out of hiding with his gun blazing.

From his jail cell, Harris told a reporter his side of the story, including that he and Effie had been married for eight years and had two children, a son and a daughter. "I do not regret the deed," he said. "If it was [possible] to do over, I would do the same thing."

Of course, the press wanted to know what Effie—described as "a rather handsome woman with beautiful form and very attractive manners"—thought about all of this. She assured the press that she was perfectly innocent: "Mr. Harris has been insanely jealous of Mr. Merritt and also everyone else with whom I have ever associated. We have lived apart much of our married life because of this insane jealousy. He has threatened others besides Mr. Merritt." She added, "The statements which you say have been made by Mr. Harris to the effect that there had been improper relations between Mr. Merritt and me are absolutely false. He never kissed me, as Mr. Harris charges, or made any other improper advances." She said the same in another interview the next day.

While he was convinced on the day of the murder that he had done the right thing, after a cooling-off period, Harris seemed to be sorry he took such drastic action. So remarked a reporter on July 10. While a few observers thought Harris acted too rashly, the majority believed he had every right to fill Merritt with as much lead as he pleased, thanks to the "unwritten law," the concept that the despoiler of a marriage deserved whatever punishment the offended party dealt. As the mainstream opinion suggests, the Harris-Merritt shooting was seen right away as an unwritten law case. Yet there were a few nagging details that must be settled: Had Merritt actually had an adulterous relationship with Mrs. Harris, and if so, could it be proved? Then there was the fact that Harris did not habitually carry a gun. He killed Merritt with a weapon he had borrowed from a friend that morning, which suggested premeditation and implied that Harris had not just happened to see Merritt walking to the park; rather, it suggested that Harris was in pursuit and gunning for him.

In a third statement to press, Effie said that she would begin divorce proceedings against Jacob right away, and she reiterated, "[B]efore God, I never committed any wrong." But interestingly, on July 12, Harris's defense team vowed that they would produce "sensational evidence"—in fact, they promised that the examining trial, to begin July 15, would "be one of the most sensational ever called in Fayette County." The day before the trial started, Effie quietly slunk out of Lexington and headed for Shelby

County—a telling sign. Also, she didn't attend the trial, even though she was under a $100 bond to do so. She was wise to slip away, as embarrassing facts came out during the proceedings:

1. Jacob Harris wasn't the only person in the family consumed with jealousy. Mrs. Harris had been angered when her boss Mr. Merritt *also* courted her sister Ireland and wanted her to be his stenographer.

2. The Harrises and Merritt had lived in the same boardinghouse from May to mid-June 1897, and there, Merritt's libidinous attentions to Effie were so obvious to all that the scandalized landlady ordered the Harrises to move out.

3. The behavior of Merritt and Mrs. Harris was so public that Harris's own sister-in-law, the aforementioned and beautifully named Gussie, had told him, "She is going to the dogs as fast as she can, and if you don't put a stop to it, everyone will know of it."

Thomas Merritt. *Louisville Courier-Journal*, July 11, 1897. *Courtesy of the* Louisville Courier-Journal.

These revelations implied that Harris had had good reason to be suspicious of Merritt. His friends and family visited his cell and reassured him that he did the right and honorable thing.

Public opinion turned palpably away from Effie. It seemed that the unwritten law would win Harris an acquittal for sure. And so it did. On July 16, Judge D. Gray Falconer dismissed Harris from custody, and the grand jury refused to indict him.

The national press was not in favor of the decision, by and large. For example, the *New York World* remarked, "[The unwritten law] is a defense not recognized by law, but custom stronger than law has made it valid not only in Kentucky, but in nearly every state in the union.…[I]t seems impossible to get a jury to convict the 'injured husband' who kills."

And then Jacob Harris did something in mid-December that was perhaps romantically correct but legally stupid. It completely turned public sentiment against him. What was his unforgivable deed? He forgave Effie and returned to her, thus making the members of the legal system who set him free look like a bunch of chumps. The Fayette County grand jury immediately reindicted Harris for murdering Merritt. "[I]t is now believed that he will fare badly at the hands of a trial jury," remarked the *Courier-Journal*. Nevertheless, Harris was released on a $4,000 bond on December 24. What the hey, it was Christmastime.

Harris faced the circuit court in April 1898. "[I]t is believed Harris will get a light sentence," opined the *Courier-Journal*. He didn't get even that. On April 7, Harris was acquitted again, the jury having opted once more to uphold the unwritten law. As others have lamented: if only juries would be so fastidious in maintaining *written* laws.

10

WANTED ALIVE, NOT DEAD

A thirty-one-year-old Black farmhand, Newton Chenault, aka Newt, was said to be a Spanish-American War veteran. While this is possible, he would have to have enlisted in his very early teens. In 1915, he lived in Donerail, about ten miles from Lexington. His great ambition in life was to marry the sixteen-year-old daughter of Luther Hummons (or Hummins), nicknamed "the mayor of Hummonsville" and described glowingly by the press as "a well-known colored citizen" and "a substantial, hard-working citizen well thought of" by Black and White residents alike. When Chenault eagerly ran the idea past Hummons, the response was something along the lines of, "Over my dead body." On October 1, Chenault even threatened to steal the girl away, only to face the father's ire.

Bright and early the next morning, Chenault borrowed a double-barreled shotgun from his employer, George Wilhoit, explaining that he was going to shoot a rabbit.

He returned a few minutes later, telling Wilhoit, "I got the rabbit all right." But he told the womenfolk at the place the truth about what he had just done on the road to Yarnallton. Then he fled. When Chenault was last seen, he was heading for Lexington.

Unfortunately for him, a witness named James White saw the whole thing, and soon, a manhunt sought Chenault. He got only a brief head start, plus he was hard to miss in a crowd, being well over six feet tall. His description was recorded on one thousand postcards that were then sent throughout the county, and they were also featured in an advertisement in the *Lexington*

Herald. The governor offered a $200 reward (over $3,500 in modern currency) for Chenault's apprehension, arrest and conviction. Yet he disappeared like the morning mist—a matter of some wonder to law enforcement (including Lexington officers and county police), not to mention the citizens, who were terrified at the possibility of Chenault turning up when least expected.

Chenault remained underground and silent until March 1916. He was killed in Hamilton, Ohio, when he tried to hold up a man who shot him instead. The justice of the peace in that city wired Lexington to inquire about that $200 reward, only to be told that the "dead body of Chenault is of no value to Kentucky." After all, the payment was specifically for the murderer's apprehension, arrest and conviction, and Chenault had not been apprehended, arrested or convicted. Always read the fine print!

11

HOW TO SCARE YOUR FIANCÉE

Harry Hatterick, merely twenty-one years old, a Lexington resident and a former inmate of the Kentucky House of Reform, was due to marry Ann Williams in only two weeks. Then on December 20, 1929, he did something stupid that cast a shadow over their plans.

Ann and her sixteen-year-old sister, Alice, both lived at 333 Lexington Avenue. They were strolling down that street when Harry approached, shirtless and with a gun in hand. He fired twice at a telephone pole beside them from seventy-five feet away. That's what he said he was aiming at, anyway. Somehow, Alice got shot in the thigh.

Harry never explained, then or later, why he fired at an object so near his fiancée and her sister. Was he just trying to scare them? Did he think they would appreciate that a hilarious prankster would soon be joining the family? Perchance Bigfoot was lurking behind the young ladies? Why shoot *twice*, anyway?

A passing laundry truck driver picked up Alice, Ann and Harry and booked it for the hospital. On the way there, Harry did another strange thing, as though he had not dealt enough surprises for one day. He aimed his gun at his own head and fired. His life was spared when the alarmed driver struck his hand just in time to throw off his aim, making a bullet hole in the truck's roof. The driver and his assistant wrestled the gun away from Hatterick.

Alice's artery was severed, and she bled to death at the hospital despite prompt medical attention. Harry was taken to jail and held without bond.

One account says he was "overcome with emotion" when he received the tragic news. Conversely, another claims Harry made a strangely unapologetic remark to a reporter: "Murder! Isn't that a hell of a charge? Well, all I know is that I was shooting at a pole and not at the girls."

He refused to clarify why he thought a public street, with two humans in the general vicinity, was a proper place to display his marksmanship. He also wouldn't comment on his reason for attempting self-annihilation. This was the most he ever had to say about it:

> *I had called Ann over the telephone and she asked me about a Christmas savings bank book I had been keeping for her. I told her I had the book, but that I didn't think we would have time to take it to the bank today. After the telephone conversation, I saw the two girls coming along Lexington Avenue, and when I was about seventy-five feet from them, I fired two shots at a telephone pole. I thought I had hit the pole, but I guess I didn't.*

No, we guess not! A possibly revealing moment came when an officer asked Harry's badly shaken fiancée, Ann, about the accident.

> *Officer: Do you think Harry was aiming at Alice?*
> *Ann: No.*
> *Officer: Do you think he was aiming at* you*?*
> *Ann:* [No answer.]

The victim's mother, Mary, said that the engaged couple "had many quarrels and a great deal of trouble" and claimed that Harry habitually carried a pistol.

Alice was buried on December 22. Harry spent the day playing cards with his new pals in jail. Ann said the Williams family believed it was an accidental shooting and that they would stand by Harry—all except Ann's father, interestingly. Harry was refused permission to attend Alice's funeral, and one suspects that the sisters' father put his foot down.

On the last day of 1929, seven prisoners broke out of the Fayette County Jail. Sixteen others, including Harry, were captured before they could flee. This incident did not make anyone think better of him.

On January 31, 1930, Hatterick was indicted on a charge of carrying a concealed weapon. If he didn't go to jail for murder or manslaughter, it seemed he would be going to jail for *something*.

Harry's trial began on February 4. On the same day, the jury voted for acquittal after forty-one minutes. That was hardly the end of the matter. The jury had reached its verdict so quickly that suspicions arose. No one raised charges of bribery, it appears, but it was suggested that the jury was prejudiced in the prisoner's favor, since one member "signaled the decision… to members of the Hatterick family before the report was read by a court official in open court." There are no details about what exactly this meant. Perhaps a jury member was observed giving the Hattericks a friendly wink and a thumbs up. In any case, the allegations were serious enough to warrant a grand jury investigation.

The jurymen were summoned to appear in court on February 11. The press doesn't say much about any hot water the jury found itself in. However, Harry Hatterick was indicted again, this time for perjury, besides that arraignment for carrying a concealed weapon. He was charged with lying under oath three times:

1. He had denied arguing with Ann at any time during the past six months. Instead, investigators discovered that Harry had quite the hair-trigger temper, just as Ann's mother said. The couple "had quarreled constantly." Once, Harry disconnected a telephone in a fit of rage. He tore up a photograph of himself and destroyed gifts he had given Ann. Also, he was known to have previously drawn a gun on her.

2. He swore under oath that he placed his pistol in his pocket the night before he shot Alice and had forgotten about it. Statements proved the contrary, as he had carried the gun at least two nights before Alice's death.

3. Then the biggie: there *was no telephone pole* in the area where he shot at the girls. It is surprising that it took so long for someone to check out this basic element of his alibi.

Harry had been acquitted of Alice's death but could still be tried on other charges. Nevertheless, was Alice's death the result of murder or manslaughter? Harry insisted the shooting was unintentional. However, one scenario makes the most sense: he intended to shoot his fiancée, with whom he did not get along and whom he had threatened with a gun before, but hit her sister instead and tried to kill himself a few minutes later. If so, Alice's death really *was* an accident, in a sense.

But Ann must have been convinced otherwise, as she married Harry in Covington on February 14, Valentine's Day. But what a lovely day that is for a wedding! The newlyweds moved to Cincinnati.

Despite being on his honeymoon, Hatterick was scheduled to go on trial on April 8 for perjury and carrying a concealed weapon. On April 23, the jury hearing the perjury charges was deadlocked and dismissed. One wonders why. The telephone pole Harry claimed he was shooting at was either there or it wasn't, and if it wasn't there, he had no reason to shoot in the sisters' direction. He had no discernible reason to shoot if the pole *had* been there, for that matter. Harry was scheduled to be tried again—plus he still had to face the concealed weapon accusation—at the next term of court. But it appears that he wasn't.

Let's hope the Hattericks enjoyed a happy life together.

12

A HUNGRY HORSE, AND WHAT THE SAUSAGE VENDOR SAW

A book on Lexington must include a horse story. I believe it is a law.

The press spelled the victim's name in various ways, including Driesbach, Dieback and Diesbach. Although he has no headstone, Diesback appears to be the correct rendition, as that is how it was spelled on his calling card. He was about forty-eight years old and from Watsontown, Pennsylvania, and this is the story of how he came to be buried in an unmarked plot in Lexington Cemetery.

Frank Spellman's Traveling Circus achieved a measure of fame around 1917 as the first motorized circus—that is, it was the first to journey from point A to point B via automobiles, rather than by horses or railroads. About a decade before, the circus was famous for a much less wholesome reason.

Stephen A. Diesback traveled with the circus as the owner of "Tiny Mite," the smallest horse in the world at only eighteen inches tall and weighing thirty-one pounds. On August 15, 1908, the show was on exhibition at the Bluegrass Fairgrounds. Diesback had a bad habit of carrying money in his socks and a worse habit of letting people know about it. "Pickpockets can't get it there," he would say slyly. "And who would think of looking in my socks?"

Someone *did* think of it, however, and sneaked into the horse trainer's tent while he was asleep. The thief shot him in the head and then bludgeoned him with a three-foot-long tent peg, which he left behind. (Readers of my book *Bizarre Bluegrass* will recall that tent pegs were cherished weapons among circus folk.) One side of Diesback's head was entirely crushed, and his brains had been beaten out. A reporter noted that when the killer swung the peg, he must have missed Tiny Mite by inches.

The other employees of the fair didn't know Diesback was dead, and as he lay stiffening in his quarters, all the other tents were struck and carted away. He seemed in danger of being left behind. Andrew Hickey, a twelve-year-old Lexington boy whom Diesback had hired to help while the show was in town, found the body the next day around noon. The victim's socks were turned inside out, and the killer had gotten away with an estimated $200. "The pony was probably the only witness to one of the most brutal murders that has occurred here in years," wrote a melodramatic reporter. Certainly, the horse was loyal to the end. He was found nosing his master's body and whinnying.

The suddenly homeless pony was cared for at Tattersall's livery stable, where the proprietors discovered that Tiny Mite was so small because his late owner had chronically underfed him. Once he had a chance to consume all the hay he wanted, the pony made himself sick from overeating.

Right from the start, suspicion centered on an unknown young man Diesback had hired to act as his "spieler" (carnival barker, that is). No one had seen him since the murder. Henry Brown, a Lexington sausage vendor, had kept his lunch counter at the fairgrounds even after the show was over, hoping to sell viands to the departing showmen. Diesback had bought a sausage around 1:00 a.m. on the night of August 15 and walked away. A couple hours later, a stranger in his shirtsleeves bought a sandwich while confiding, "That's the last nickel I've got, but there's a fellow over here owes me money, and I've got to have it before daylight." The talkative customer departed, and not long afterward, Brown heard a muffled shot, which he attributed to the show's cowboys. A half hour later, the stranger returned, this time with his coat on. He purchased two sandwiches and made tracks.

Well, perhaps Brown met the killer. But his story sounds a lot like the marvelous things we tend to remember after some dramatic event. It is unlikely that a red-handed killer would purchase something from a witness who might remember him, especially so soon before and after committing murder.

The police were still interested in the missing barker, finally identified as Harold Lamble, whose father, H.V. Lamble, was Diesback's business partner. The elder Lamble arrived in Lexington from Macon, Georgia, on August 18 to prove his partial ownership of Tiny Mite and was thunderstruck to discover that his son had vanished and was suspected of murder.

On August 19, Governor Willson offered a $500 reward (nearly $10,500 today) for Diesback's killer. The next day, the showman was buried in Lexington Cemetery by Lamble Sr. and members of the fraternal organization the Improved Order of Red Men. Mr. Lamble didn't want to believe his son capable of murder:

> *I do not understand Harold's disappearance. My idea about the matter is that he has gone ahead to the next place where he and Diesback were to show and that he has erected a platform there and is waiting. He had no reason for committing such a crime, as I had been giving him so much money each week besides his expenses, and I am an easy father, in a way....I do not understand it at all and am sorely puzzled and almost heartbroken.*

Lamble was not found. In April 1911, the governor renewed the reward, this time for only $100, and a *Lexington Herald* article from July 1911 on the laxity of criminal punishment states, "Harold Lamble, who committed murder at the Bluegrass Fair three years ago, has never been apprehended." So, Lamble escaped the law's clutches—maybe.

On August 22, 1918, in Rahway, New Jersey, Arthur Kupfer and his fiancée, Edith Janny, picked up two hitchhikers, who killed them and stole their car. In July 1920, a tip led police to two men who were being held in New York's Auburn Penitentiary: Charles Perchand, imprisoned on a weapons charge, and George Brandon, convicted of grand larceny. Brandon's real name was Harold Lamble.

Perchand and Lamble were extradited to New Jersey. Perchand turned state's evidence and saved his life, but Lamble was tried for double homicide and found guilty. Lamble got the chair on August 23, 1921, and I don't mean an antique Hepplewhite.

Was the killer of Kupfer and Janny the same Harold Lamble who was suspected of murdering Stephen Diesback in 1908? According to Auburn Prison records, the Lamble who got in trouble in New Jersey in 1919–20 was born in Brooklyn in 1891. If he was the same man who fled from the circus, he would have been seventeen at the time, and the missing Lamble was described as a "young man." The birthplace/hometown of the 1908 Lamble is uncertain, though his father lived in Georgia. It is not impossible, of course, for the elder Lamble to have moved from New York to Georgia at some point. So, the killers may have been the same man, or perhaps the United States was infested with two murderous Harold Lambles at roughly the same time.

An older Harold Lamble. Was he the killer of Stephen Diesback? *Central New Jersey Home News*, July 20, 1920. *Courtesy of* Central New Jersey Home News.

As for the horse Tiny Mite—because I like to be thorough about these things—representatives of Diesback's estate sold him at auction in Lexington on September 10, 1908, to James Watkins, the president of the Bluegrass Fair, who hopefully fed him better than Diesback did. The $550 proceeds went to the murdered man's widow, Minnie, back in Watsontown. At some point, circus owner Spellman purchased the horse, so Tiny Mite returned to the show. But Kentucky twice brought bad luck to him. The nine-year-old horse died on April 14, 1909, at the Southern Electrical and Industrial Exposition at the Louisville Armory. Spellman vowed to have him taxidermized so that his wonder might live on. Perhaps Tiny Mite, who saw a human murdered only inches away, exists yet in a warehouse, museum or attic.

13

NO STOPPING HENRY!

On March 5, 1845, Lexington's Clifton R. Thomson, Esq.—can't neglect that important title, as it means its bearer is entitled to practice law—was sitting in the courthouse at Mount Sterling, Montgomery County, engaged in a lawsuit against his brother-in-law, former Congressman Henry Daniel. There's no word about who was suing whom or precisely what the suit concerned.

According to an eyewitness, Thomson's lawyers "exposed the rascality of old Harry," a man "of infamous notoriety." A furious Daniel stood up and demanded to know if Thomson had authorized his counsel to speak of him that way. When Thomson confirmed it, Daniel drew a pistol and shot him dead on the spot, right there in the courtroom. "Thus has fallen, by the hand of violence, one of Fayette's most gifted, noble, generous, and honorable sons," lamented the *Lexington Inquirer*.

"The court ordered the old fiend to jail instanter, and it is hoped that the day of his receipt of justice is not far off," remarked correspondent Samuel A. Young. Note that even in 1845, Daniel was referred to as "old" and "notorious." Before it was all over, he would become even older and more infamous.

Daniel's wife, after hearing her husband had murdered her brother, went insane less than a week after the tragedy.

The murder trial began on June 16. The judge who was supposed to preside, Kenaz Farrow, recused himself since he had witnessed the murder and was replaced with Judge Lusk. Despite all those courtroom witnesses who saw the shooting up close and personal, it was obvious from the beginning that the prosecution would lose the case. A jury was found and empaneled in only three hours, a suspiciously quick time considering the seriousness of the charge. A journalist found the jury's political makeup lopsided: "eleven [Locofocos] and one Whig." In modern terms, that's eleven proto-Democrats and one proto-Republican. Daniel happened to be a "Locofoco," that is, a Democrat. Hearing of this, the *Louisville Journal* remarked:

> [W]*e deem it perfectly certain that Daniel, like most or all other mid-day assassins in the West and South, will go unpunished. We fear it is too true that, in some parts of our country, there is in effect no law against assassination, provided the assassin has the audacity and recklessness to perpetrate the murder publicly and before the eyes of scores or hundreds or thousands.*

A few months later, the same paper remarked that at least South Carolina was willing to execute its public murderers: "At Greenville, two or three weeks ago, a gentleman who had gone into the street and openly and boldly shot another gentleman dead, was convicted of murder and sentenced to be hung."

The predictions were correct: Daniel was acquitted after the jury deliberated for only two hours. Aghast at the decision, the *Journal* remarked, "*He did shoot his brother-in-law*, and not all the courts, juries, and arguments in the world can destroy that fact." Then the paper mentioned, perhaps suggestively, a recent case from another county in which residents had lynched a prisoner because they were sure the courts would not deal with him justly. The paper reiterated in October, "[I]f he is not a murderer, there is no murder upon the face of the broad earth….The decision of the jury… is a disgrace to Kentucky."

Getting away with a barefaced public homicide might be a life triumph enough for most men, but Henry Daniel was undaunted. In June 1855, he hit the headlines after he was married in Mount Sterling at over seventy years old. He died on October 5, 1873, at the age of eighty-seven. He was so old that Kentucky wasn't a state when he was born. Few official biographies mention his little brush with the law, although that was what he was most famous for in life, rather than his stint in the U.S. House of Representatives and his captaincy in the War of 1812.

14

THE HONEYMOON IS OVER

In the summer of 1851, a fellow named Harper (*not* from Lexington, the papers emphasized) became entranced with a young lady in the city. Her name was Merrill, and she had seen only fifteen summers. Harper took her to Aberdeen in Butler County and married her. Within weeks, the missus sought a divorce. They were legitimately married, it appears, but for reasons known only to himself, Harper enjoyed making people think they weren't. "It was a sham marriage," he would sneer and then cast aspersions on his wife's morals, and he probably tweaked the ends of his moustache like a stereotypical stage villain while he said it.

The brand-new Mrs. Harper did not take kindly to being made a public fool, and she begged her brother and brother-in-law to settle Mr. Harper's hash. Both demurred. She was going to have to save her reputation and honor herself. So, on July 7, she prowled the town's streets dressed in black and wearing a veil for a disguise, looking for her oaf of a husband with a suspiciously heavy bulge in her pocket.

When she spotted her prey on Main Street, she sneaked up behind him, yanked out a pistol, aimed it at his head and tried to pull the trigger. Luckily for Harper, the weapon was half-cocked and wouldn't go off. Mrs. Harper corrected the problem and aimed again. Someone shouted, "Look out!" just before she fired, causing the oblivious Harper to turn slightly. It saved his life. She put three buckshot in Harper's arm and back and, thinking him dead, promised to turn herself in to a magistrate. But then she realized he had mere flesh wounds and figured that if she was going to surrender to the authorities anyway, it might as well be for a good reason. She produced a second pistol and chased him after asking bystanders if she had their kind permission to kill him. He proved fleeter of foot and hid.

When Lexingtonians heard the story, they sympathized with the young Mrs. Harper and vowed to lynch her man—if they could find him. They couldn't, because by nightfall, he had abandoned the city, never to be seen again as far as the record shows.

The *Lexington Reporter and Observer* reported and observed, "If the reports which have reached us are true, the lady has had ample cause for this desperate attempt at revenge for injuries inflicted." Whatever Harper said about his wife, it was *bad*.

15

DAVID'S BOWIE, OR: DON'T FEAR THE REPERCUSSIONS

Dr. David C. Sullivan was from Georgetown, Scott County, and Henry Twyman was from Woodford County. Patrick Meehan, a young man who had recently moved to Lexington, was a clerk in a carpet and furniture store. Sullivan and Twyman got roaring drunk in the city on October 1, 1851. Somehow, somewhere, Sullivan lost his cloak, and the pair staggered hither and yon searching for it.

They wobbled into Hollenkamp's confectionery, and by unlucky chance, Meehan was there. A dialogue something like the following ensued:

> *Sullivan: Do you have my cloak? Did I leave it here?*
> *Meehan: I don't have it, and I don't know if you left it here.*
> *Sullivan:* [In the fashion of newspapers at the time] *You're a d—d liar!*
> *Twyman: Hey, Sullivan, do you have a knife?*
> *Sullivan: No.*
> *Twyman: Here's my Bowie. Kill him!*

Sullivan was open to suggestions, and he stabbed Meehan in the heart. The wounded youth took a couple of steps and died. Considering William Weigart's murder of a clerk named Cushing in a different Lexington confectionery two years later for "insulting his wife," one wonders why the town's candy stores bred such mayhem.

The *Lexington Statesman* took the occasion to editorialize against concealed weapons but added that if legislation could not solve the problem, perhaps all citizens should go armed so they could get the drop on others with murderous intent:

> *A peaceable man in the present condition of things may feel himself compelled to bear arms as a measure of protection against the violent; but he who secretly bears them in the absence of this motive evinces the malevolence of an assassin, and the law should be so framed that, should he kill with such* [a] *weapon, he should be tried as an assassin and executed by hanging.*

The cold-blooded murder created "a most profound sensation in this community," added the paper. A week later, some papers reported that would-be lynchers determined to hang Dr. Sullivan and Twyman on the spot if the examining court permitted them to have bail. Fortunately for the prisoners, the court decreed otherwise. The *Statesman* denied any such mob action. It called the story a "slander" and said that citizens wanted the law to take its course and that the rumor "was without any substantial foundation in fact." But the phrase "without any *substantial* foundation" as opposed to "no foundation" suggests that there may have been a little something to it.

The trial began in Fayette Circuit Court on August 3, 1852. Attorneys for Sullivan and Twyman asked for a change of venue, which was granted. After the usual delays, the trial proper began in Georgetown in September. This was one case in which the change of venue tactic may have succeeded better than anyone expected. Sullivan was from Georgetown, after all, and the hometown jury acquitted him despite overwhelming evidence, and they also granted Twyman the possibility of bail. And bailed he was—until the next court term. The Scott Countians acquitted him, too, in March 1853. Both men then dropped out of history, having escaped dropping through a gallows trapdoor.

16

FUN AT THE FAIR

Let's go back in time and check out the Fayette County Fair of 1854. An overly educated correspondent with the pseudonym Se De Kay (Hey, do you suppose his initials were C.D.K.?) sent the *Louisville Courier* verbose reports about the celebration. Most of the news concerned who won prizes for the best quilts, coverlets, embroidery, cattle, tobacco and dozens of other categories. Many pickpockets were present, but no one appreciated their hard-earned skills. Attendees who may have thought exhibitions of poultry or bonnets tiresome soon witnessed livelier unscheduled events.

Thomas Buford of Woodford County whupped George H. Thomas of Mount Sterling in a fistfight. George left for town in an unpleasant mood and then returned to the fairground just after noon. Before five hundred gaping bystanders, Thomas approached Buford near the ladies' stand and fired at least four shots at him with a revolver. Buford had a gun of his own and shot back, hitting Thomas in the thigh. One of the combatants accidentally shot Dr. Sam Letcher's enslaved woman in the mouth. The bullet exited through her neck, "inflicting a very dangerous wound." It was estimated that Buford and Thomas fired at each other seven or eight times near the crowd, and when they ran out of ammo, they threw their empty guns at each other. Then they menaced one another with Bowie knives.

Thomas Ferguson of Fayette County handed George Thomas a loaded pistol. Buford's brother Charles took offense and scalped Ferguson with his own knife, and the reporter believed Charles also deprived his opponent of one eye.

Meanwhile, a volley of unaimed bullets flew into a crowd consisting mostly of women. A Black youth who was standing nearby was also hit by a stray bullet. It was considered miraculous that no one else was struck. Former governors John J. Crittenden and Robert Letcher were nearby when the action commenced, and both fled with impressive, even awe-inspiring, speed.

All this anarchy happened in a single day, September 14, 1854. Se De Kay still found pompous compliments to say about the fair.

"Such scenes of violence are of too common occurrence in Kentucky," editorialized the *Courier*. "And it is to be hoped the authorities of Lexington will make an example of the guilty parties." Buford, Thomas and the newly hairless Ferguson were summoned before the Fayette County Court on September 21. They were bound over at the sum of $2,000 and ordered to keep the peace for a year. This wasn't the temperamental Thomas Buford's last serious scrape with the law. To find out what happened to him several years later, see my book *Murder in Old Kentucky*.

17

AN ENTIRE CIVIL WAR LATER

And now, a story about what could happen when you open a door. On the night of Thursday, May 26, 1859, Alexander Warren of Madison County entered Megowan's Hotel in Lexington. "Can you direct me to the boardinghouse where Captain Benjamin Blincoe lives?" he asked. An obliging individual gave him directions and probably regretted his helpfulness for the rest of his life.

After he arrived at the boardinghouse, Warren walked upstairs to the second floor. It was 10:30 p.m. He woke Blincoe, the Fayette County jailer, by pounding on the door. Blincoe opened it and asked what Warren wanted at such a late hour.

"Somebody wants to kill me, or I have to kill somebody," Warren explained. Blincoe, realizing his visitor might not be mentally sound, humored him, saying, "Nobody wants to kill you. You should go now." In the night's second unfortunate act of generosity, he offered to help his unwanted caller find the way out. The two men and Mrs. Blincoe walked down the hall, with Mr. Blincoe carrying a candle, when Warren turned and opened a side door.

"That's not the exit," said Blincoe. Warren responded by knocking the candlestick from the jailer's hand, stabbing him six times and slashing his abdomen, leaving his victim's intestines partially hanging out and plopping onto the corridor's floor—an unpleasant sight for all concerned, especially Mrs. Blincoe, who saw what had happened to her husband after she relit the candle. Her shrieks alerted a passerby outside, Mr. Richardson, who hurried to the scene. As he approached, he saw Warren stick his head through the open outer door. The assassin ran back inside and hid in a room. Richardson trapped him by simply leaning against the door.

When the police let Warren out of the room to arrest him, Warren and Blincoe both muttered incoherently, the former out of seeming insanity, the latter from pain. "Why did you do this?" asked an officer.

"He killed my Negro, so I killed him," said Warren. "Here is the knife I did it with." He surrendered a needle-sharp, brand-new weapon.

Blincoe died the following night at 10:20 p.m., having survived his injuries for almost twenty-four hours. The death, oddly, was reported along with the city's racing news. Warren had problems of his own when a mob gathered around the jail. The authorities took the situation very seriously; after all, a year before, a mob had lynched William Barker for killing City Marshal Joseph Beard. Distinguished citizens urged the crowds who were hankering for Warren's blood to disperse peacefully—just as they had pleaded in vain in for Barker. The furious mob left after Judge Goodloe promised he would try the prisoner without delay on May 29. But *really*, they were probably cowed by the 150 hastily sworn-in deputies and the Lexington Rifles, a military unit sent to guard Warren's hide. Despite these precautions, the city was in a state of chaos. Every street swarmed with angry persons "hurrying to and fro," seemingly for some sinister purpose, said an eyewitness. The authorities stretched taut ropes across Short Street, near the jail, to prevent unauthorized carriages from approaching. That was the nineteenth-century equivalent of those Stinger spike strips modern police toss on the highway to deflate the tires of getaway cars. Rumors spread that Warren would be snatched and hanged at any moment, and the roads into the city were clogged with country folks who wouldn't have missed seeing a real lynching for anything else the world had to offer. They trudged home with blighted hopes when they learned that Warren was as safe as the crown jewels in the jail that had once been supervised by his victim.

Handbills appeared asking residents to meet at the courthouse on Saturday, May 28, and this was generally understood to be a call to a lynching. The courthouse was where Barker had been hanged the previous year. At nightfall, the courthouse bell rang, and excited people hurried to the scene. To their disappointment, they were greeted by only sensible community leaders, including John C. Breckinridge, Reverend S.L. Hanson and Roger W. Hanson—Hanson had tried to be a voice of reason at the Barker lynching, too—who urged the crowd to let the law take its course. Most slunk away, but a few brave souls tried to rush the jail. They gave up after the Lexington Guards offered persuasive, double-barreled reasons to leave Warren alone. One of the men who warded off these marauders was Captain John Hunt Morgan, soon to become one of Kentucky's most famous Confederate cavalry officers and raiders.

It turned out that the greatest danger to Warren was himself. On the morning of August 4, he cut his own throat in his cell. Physicians thought he would soon be measured for cerements, but Warren proved to be better at killing other people. Despite Judge Goodloe's vow to the first mob that Warren would be tried immediately, he wasn't scheduled go to the courtroom until June 1860, a year later.

Even before Warren was tried, people speculated about his sanity or lack of the same. The *Observer and Reporter* thought he was faking it: "[T]he morning after the occurrence Warren acted and talked like an insane man, but whether this was an assumption [an act, that is] or not remains to be developed. The transaction itself certainly bore not the air of insanity, for there was more of method in it, from first to last, than usually accompanies the doings of a madman."

Insanity aside, folks wondered about Warren's motive. His statement that Blincoe had "killed his Negro" never came up at trial or at any other time, so it was presumably investigated and found to be nonsense. Some believed the purpose of Warren's act was to create a distraction so a prisoner could be sprung from Blincoe's jail, but no one escaped that night. Besides, Blincoe was home that night, not at the prison, so what was to keep the theoretical convict from escaping without a distraction?

Warren's attorneys requested and received a change of venue to Mercer County, likely on the grounds that Fayette Countians might annihilate him. But the Mercer Jail must not have been as well-guarded as the one in Fayette. In 1860, Warren strolled away from the place in broad daylight, as though he was out to gather strawberries. On July 6, 1865, a man named Brink nabbed him in Winchester, Clark County. Warren had drawn attention to himself by getting drunk, and after some toughs gave him a comprehensive beating, he unwisely boasted, "I'll kill you all just as I killed Blincoe!" He was back in Lexington a few hours after his capture and stored in poor Blincoe's jail. No one menaced him this time around.

Finally! Several years and an entire civil war later—and after two more lengthy legal delays—Warren was tried in Harrodsburg, Mercer County, on November 22, 1866. Two days later, he was acquitted, although he had murdered Blincoe in front of his wife, been found standing at the scene with the bloody knife and never denied his action. He pleaded not guilty due to insanity, and the jury believed him. He soon took up quarters at the asylum in Hopkinsville. Why he chose Blincoe, of all people, as the person he "had to kill," no one ever found out.

Maybe Warren was genuinely insane, but someone else *definitely* was. As with so many historical true crime stories, Warren's saga includes a bitter, unexpected aftermath. Sally Griffith, Blincoe's daughter, was only seventeen when her father was disemboweled, and she never recovered from the shock. In August 1875, she was declared insane. Several men on the jury that declared her insane remembered the excitement that prevailed in the city after her father's death.

18

CHEATING THE HANGMAN OF HIS FEE

John Bryant of Powell County was likely a chronic domestic abuser. His final act of violence against his wife was his worst. In April 1870, he stabbed her in the heart with such force that he cut it in half. Her baby was nearly smothered in the pool of blood. To give Bryant a modicum of credit, he immediately regretted it. He surrendered to the authorities without delay, refused to hire an attorney, pleaded guilty and said he wanted to be hanged as long as he was given ten days to write a full confession. No, Bryant didn't mind being hanged. But when his end came, he probably would have preferred that a professional did the job rather than a pack of rank amateurs.

Bryant must have been granted a change of venue, as we next see him awaiting trial in the Lexington Jail in February 1871, when the city must have been a real carnival of crime. Bryant was confined along with thirty-one other prisoners, including a rapist, a forger and four men charged with murder. The rest were in the slammer for grand larceny. Bryant was the only White prisoner, which might tell us something about "disproportionate" racially based arrests of the period—but what should be considered proportionate? Ponder the question, I beg you.

In March, Bryant was sent back to Powell for trial. It would have been better for all concerned if he had remained in Lexington. On Friday, March 31, at least fifty masked men approached the jail at Stanton. They behaved differently than the usual lynchers in a couple of ways. Most of the time, a murderer's greatest danger of being mobbed came just after the crime or within a few days of it; after a few weeks or months, tempers cooled, and the killer was left to the mercy of a judge and jury. But in this case, even the passing of an entire year didn't help Bryant.

The mob informed Mr. Combs, the jailer, that he must hand over the prisoner. Words failed to convince him, but their cocked pistols did. Bryant was sought, found and, wearing only his pants, taken to Judy's Creek, about a quarter of a mile from the jail. His last known words were, "May God have mercy on me." The next morning, passersby saw the unlovely sight of Bryant hanging from a tree limb.

The other circumstance that made this mob unusual was that seeing Bryant suspended between heaven and Earth awakened poetic feelings in one lyncher, who left behind a verse complete with a dedication:

Dedicated to John Bryant, who Murdered His Wife

'Tis a beautiful night,
And with calm delight
I gaze on the glorious scene.
The sun goes to rest,
Wreathing the calm on West,
While John Bryant's tears
Are falling on his breast.
The bright and happy hours of Bryant are o'er;
The shadow of his life is flitting before.
So farewell to the world. I bid it adieu:
I'll make my amends in another in view.
For the many cruel deeds I've committed through life,
I'm brought to the Gallows for the murder of my wife;
The Gents who have me in custody to-night,
I say to you all, have served me just right.

Then came the postscript:

He requests to be buried where his brother is.
He is to be left here until 10 o'clock to-morrow.
—K.K.K.

A literary critic might admire the startling shift in point of view from a first-person narrator to Bryant himself in line 10 and then reverting to the narrator in line 16. Given Bryant's eagerness to die for his crime, perhaps he would have agreed with the sentiment expressed in lines 14 and 15. His trial was scheduled to begin on July 1, and doubtless, he would have been executed anyway.

The mob's note demanded that Bryant's body remain where it was until 10:00 a.m., but it wasn't cut down until 11:00 a.m. Saturday morning. Likely, the wary citizenry wanted to play it safe. Bryant was "buried where his brother is," as mentioned in the poem, in Estill County.

19

RASHOMON IN KENTUCKY, OR: CHOOSE YOUR REALITY

Rashomon is a classic 1950 Japanese film directed by Akira Kurosawa, in which a case of rape and murder is retold from multiple contradictory perspectives. We like to say, "I trust only what I see with my own eyes." But the film suggests that our point of view is so influenced by our own fallibility that even what we see cannot be trusted. A notorious historic Kentucky murder begs the question asked over two thousand years ago by Pontius Pilate (and again much later by Johnny Cash): "What is truth?" Contemplate the different angles of the Parker case, and then you can be the judge. There will be confusion. It is unavoidable.

Fittingly, the press couldn't even agree on the victim's name. Was it John Wills, Will, Willet, Willets, Willetts or Willis? The most common variant was Wills, so we shall stick with it. Everyone agreed he was too young to die at only eighteen, and everyone agreed that the culprit was his former employer, Montgomery Hobbs Parker Sr., who lived a few miles from Lexington.

Version One

Parker, a fifty-year-old prominent, wealthy farmer and stock dealer, had hired the slightly built Montgomery County teenager Wills as a manual laborer for a fee of $12.50 per month, but Wills had heard that Parker was slow to pay his workers. On September 26, 1873, after a day of cutting corn and digging potatoes, Wills went to Lexington to get an officer to accompany him to the farm to get his back wages. He didn't succeed, and the next day, he returned to the city to try again, this time accompanied by a seventeen-year-old fellow laborer named Marcus DeShong (the press also called him Deshong, Dishong and even more grotesque permutations such as Dishony). They left Parker's farm on foot with two of his brand-new corn knives and his favorite dog, possibly planning to sell them to recoup what the farmer owed them. They were blissfully unaware that Parker was chasing them on horseback.

At Chilesburg, eight miles from the city, Parker caught up with his workers on the pike to Winchester. The young men saw him, abandoned the road and took to a field that belonged to R. Benjamin Graves (or Groves). The earliest news accounts say that Parker fired two shots at them and missed. When he was within twenty feet of the travelers, Wills threw his hands up and begged for mercy. Parker shot him in the mouth. The bullet ranged downward and entered Wills's heart, killing him nearly instantly. Rumor held that Parker fled for Lexington after killing his worker, which was confirmed when attorney Colonel William C. Breckinridge of that city announced that Parker had hired him.

Officer George Darnaby found Parker in Lexington and arrested him. Darnaby, seemingly gifted with the ability to read minds, lodged Parker in the Megowan Hotel, not in a vermin-infested jail cell as one might expect, on the grounds that his prisoner "had no idea of escaping." This was not the only time authorities were strangely accommodating to Parker. Gossip that Wills's father and friends intended to lynch Parker proved untrue. Mr. Wills was described as "a very poor man, an honest, hard-working blacksmith" in Camargo, Montgomery County. He was too poor even to retrieve his son's body for several days.

Parker's examining trial was held in a schoolhouse at Bryant's Station, a few miles from Lexington, on October 3. The purpose of an examining trial is to determine whether the prisoner is likely guilty and *should* be tried in the first place. A reporter remarked, "The trial was set for this out-of-the-way place in accordance with Parker's wishes, and in deference to the same 'authority' two justices, Esquires Coons and Carter presided." (Note those sarcastic quotation marks!) The prisoner got to choose not only *where* he would be tried, presumably after several good days' rest in the hotel, but also *which* officials would hear the case. As far as I can tell, these circumstances were unprecedented. (The reporter included the odd and irrelevant comment that good corn couldn't grow at Bryant's Station.) An important but unnamed witness, described as one whose testimony in itself was "enough to convict the prisoner," was not present, so the proceedings were delayed until October 4.

Parker seemed to be getting his way, but then his luck turned. The trial reconvened in the Fayette County Courthouse rather than in the venue of his choice; also, he had no control over which witnesses were called against him. Worst of all, his son Montgomery Parker Jr., age eighteen, had been arrested the day before for being an accessory to the crime. While Montgomery Parker Jr. was unmentioned in the earliest accounts, he played a large role in the tragedy.

Version Two

John F. Davis of Chilesburg testified that he was at William Lowe's store on September 27, when Parker rode up on horseback and asked if he had seen two young men with corn knives pass on foot. "A Negro boy told him they had," said Davis. Davis, convinced that something dramatic was about to transpire, was determined not to miss a moment of it. He ran to a hilltop to get a better view. He estimated that he was 850 yards from the scene. He heard two shots and, moments later, saw Parker Jr. fire twice at two men running across an open field. In a panic, the pair dashed into a thicket. One ran back out into the exposed space. Parker Sr. rode after him. The young man, identified as Wills, stopped, and Parker halted his horse ten or twenty yards away. The terrified fugitive held up his hands in surrender. Parker shot Wills in the mouth, as described, and then dismounted and curiously examined the corpse he had just manufactured. He climbed back on his horse, rode a short distance and then returned, dismounted again and looked at the body a second time. Davis ran to the wounded boy, and by the time he had arrived, Clifton Crim and four young Black men were there. Davis said Wills's friend DeShong had a pistol as well as a corn knife. Davis's testimony is not easy to follow, but it sounds as though Parker Jr. fired at the youths twice and missed, and then his father rode up and killed Wills.

Version Three

Clifton Crim testified that he had been standing in the doorway of his house on the Combs Ferry Road when he saw one man running for the pasture and another on horseback a few hundred yards behind him. The man on foot stopped and turned to his pursuer. The six-hundred-yard distance was great enough that Crim could not make out what Wills said to Parker, but the pleading tone was clear. Crim did not see Parker's pistol, but he heard the shot and saw smoke. Six bystanders arrived at the shooting site at the same time, Crim estimated, including himself and Wills's friend DeShong. The victim was still breathing but for only a half-minute. Crim agreed that Parker rode away and returned to examine Wills.

Version Four

William Lowe owned the store where Wills and DeShong stopped briefly just before the Parkers caught up with them. Lowe noticed that they carried corn knives, but contrary to other witnesses, he did not see that they were dognapping. He saw Parker Jr. ineffectually fire shots in the pasture, and then he, too, witnessed the angry farmer Parker Sr. riding into the field, chasing and shooting Wills. Unlike the others present, Lowe couldn't bring himself to go to the body, but he did distantly see Parker's weird postmortem examination of Wills.

Version Five

Ed Turner, a Black laborer who lived on Lowe's property, was closer to the scene than most eyewitnesses, only between 200 and 300 yards away. (Later, he revised his estimate to 350 yards.) He was standing by an old icehouse at the Shipp place adjoining Graves's pasture when he saw Parker Sr. pursuing Wills. The teenager held up his hands and, "in a mournful tone of voice," cried out just before Parker shot him, "Please, please!" But did Parker take deliberate aim? Did the horse shy? These would become important questions. Turner testified, "I didn't notice whether Parker took aim or not. If the horse was in motion, I didn't see it. I didn't see the horse jump. I was looking at it all. If the horse was scared, I didn't notice it." Turner heard only the shot that killed Wills, not the other two allegedly fired by Parker Jr.

Version Six

Mr. Didlake witnessed the event from the front rather than from the side like the others. He saw Wills running over a hill and then Parker Sr. riding over the same. He twice heard Wills say, "Oh, please, don't shoot." Ed Turner testified that he heard Parker shout at his quarry, but Didlake didn't hear it. Parker maneuvered his horse around so that his back was to Didlake when the shot was fired. "The horse didn't scare," he added.

Version Seven

This was important testimony from DeShong, Wills's traveling companion. He admitted they took the corn knives but didn't mention the dog: "I told Wills not to take [them], but he said he might as well have them as nothing." They were walking to Winchester when Parker overtook them near Lowe's store. DeShong added that he had a gun as well as the knife, corroborating John F. Davis's statement. After Parker Jr. fired twice, DeShong fired back, but the cap burst. "We ran a short distance, and I surrendered." Parker Jr. stood guard over him as his father chased Wills.

R. Benjamin Graves said Parker Sr. had confessed to him and Mrs. Graves right after the shooting. Defense squabbled with the prosecution about the admissibility of this testimony, and just before the adjournment of the examining trial's first day, it was allowed. The next morning, October 6, the session opened with the next version of the story.

Version Eight

Parker Jr., freshly arrived in Lexington and himself under warrant as an accessory to murder, testified that on September 27, he had come home and noticed Wills, DeShong and the knives were gone, as was the valuable dog, which we now learn belonged to the son, not the father: "Pa said he wouldn't have taken $5 for it." (A modern equivalent is about $130. A later evaluation under oath placed the canine's value at $50, or $1,310 today—a dog worth having!) The Parkers mounted their horses and pursued the absconders. When they caught up, DeShong fired a shot at them and then another. Parker Jr. testified that he shot back only once and missed, but DeShong gave up. The young man added a possibly important detail: he said Wills threw his hat in the face of his father's horse, causing it to dodge. The motion threw Parker Sr. off balance, and he shot Wills in the mouth by accident. The farmer dismounted, examined the body and, according to his son, made the following remarks to Mrs. R. Benjamin Graves: "Madam, I shot a young man back yonder just now, who has been working for me. It was an accident. I took my pistol out when the boys were shooting back yonder, and forgot to put it up, and when my horse whirled it went off and shot him. I would not have had it happen for $5,000." Parker Jr. told the court that he rode to Lexington to procure a coffin from Patterson the undertaker.

Version Nine

Mrs. Graves testified that she was in her garden when she heard three to five shots. (Most witnesses heard three; some heard four.) She agreed that, at the time, the Parkers had referred to the shooting as an accident and added that Parker Sr. said, "They stole my dog and knives, and I'm taking DeShong to town. I won't be treated in that manner." When Mrs. Graves assured him that the thoroughly cowed DeShong wouldn't try anything stupid, Parker said, "He had better not!"

***

A reporter painted a none too flattering word portrait of Parker: "His head is covered with a heavy suit of iron-gray hair, while a long, rough, tangled gray beard covers the lower portion of his face. It is not a pleasant one by any means. I have known the prisoner for two or three years, and at no time have I ever been favorably impressed with it." Whether Parker's villainous appearance influenced them, the jury ruled that he must stand trial for murder. He was denied bail and had to sit in the Fayette County Jail until the November term of the circuit court. Meanwhile, Parker Jr. was allowed $100 bail, which was paid by his uncle Howard Parker.

The murder trial was supposed to begin on March 30, 1874, but that very morning, an important witness, Clifton Crim, could not be located. He supposedly had become "deranged," and his brothers hurried him off to Jericho, Henry County, for treatment. Some legal authorities whiffed a rodent, wondering why Crim couldn't get sufficient medical attention right there in Lexington, and a newspaper correspondent called Falcon noted that the witness's disappearance spawned rumors that it was wise not to repeat:

"The singular facts in regard to this spiriting away of a material witness… has excited much comment that, under the circumstances, I do not feel at liberty to give."

In keeping with the *Rashomon*-like nature of the story, here is how a reporter described Parker in March 1874, in contrast to the negative depiction by the earlier writer: "[A]n active, energetic trader….[H]e has retained his indomitable energy….He is one of a family, well-connected, well-known, and generally popular, unusually attached to each other, and very warm in their friendships….[He is] happily married to an estimable lady of Louisville, with children by a former marriage about him." This sympathetic journalist declared—on what authority, he did not reveal—that rather than Wills throwing his hat in his pursuer's horse's face, he instead waved it in the air in a gesture of surrender. But the result was the same: the horse panicked, Parker lost his equilibrium and he shot Wills by accident. Another difference: the earliest accounts implied that Parker was left free to wander the Earth as he pleased after shooting a teenager, as if his wealth and prominence made the law reluctant to deal with him until Officer Darnaby finally collared him. But this new rendition stated that Parker surrendered voluntarily after several days. The reporter noted, too, that while public opinion was strongly against Parker at first, tempers had since cooled.

At last, the trial started on April Fool's Day, and the world was treated to the following.

Versions Ten and Eleven

The prosecution argued that Parker, unwilling to pay the boys' wages and enraged that they had the temerity to filch his knives and dog, chased them on horseback several miles after they got a good head start. His son captured DeShong, and Parker cornered an unarmed Wills, whose pleadings for his life were answered with an intentionally fired bullet through his mouth.

The defense's way of seeing things was that DeShong had already fired twice at Parker and his son, so of course, Parker had his gun out and ready to fire, since, for all he knew, Wills also was armed and dangerous. Wills made an abrupt gesture at the horse, probably hoping to scare it into running or perhaps throw off its rider. Instead, the horse shied, and Parker fired by accident. No one could be positive what happened; the nearest witness, Ed Turner, was at least 350 yards away by his own estimate. Thus, there were grounds for reasonable doubt. As the two sides battled to condemn or save Parker, the jury heard further stories.

Too Many Differing Versions to Bother with Numbering

April 2 was an action-packed day—if one considers listening to witness testimony exciting. Storekeeper Lowe repeated his former testimony and added that he did not see Parker's horse flinch. Clifton Crim's temporary insanity must have been short-lived indeed, as he was present and considered sufficiently lucid to take the stand. His earlier testimony was essentially unchanged, and he also did not see the horse swerve. Naturally, Parker's defense attorney Colonel Breckinridge wanted to know more about the witness's alleged brief derangement. Crim said, "I had been bothered about this case by various persons, and my mind was troubled about it." This implies that unnamed individuals pressured him not to testify, which would explain why he was rushed out of town—but not his equally mysterious return a few days later. He was more explicit under cross-examination, revealing that he had been warned by others that General John B. Huston had threatened him with violence if he returned to Lexington to testify. Huston, like Breckinridge, was one of Parker's defense lawyers, so Breckinridge probably wished he hadn't asked a question with an answer that embarrassed a fellow attorney on his own side. So, had Huston tried to intimidate a witness? Maybe not. Because on the other hand, Crim admitted that he had "hallucinations for some time past" and "frequently thought people were hunting him when they were not."

The court heard from several previously unknown witnesses to the murder. David Carr said he had been home on the critical day, and like other observers, he saw Wills and DeShong carrying corn knives and then the Parkers in pursuit. Beverly Powell, a Black laborer—by 1874, Black people could testify against White defendants in Kentucky murder cases—ironically had been cutting corn when he saw Parker shoot Wills. Neither man's testimony added anything different or contradicted the record. Likewise, there were no new insights from the other Black witnesses, Edward Turner, William and Julian Didlake and Tom Smith.

Marcus DeShong, Wills's traveling companion, proved a strong asset to the prosecution. "His evidence covered points not touched by other witnesses," remarked a reporter, "and if uncontradicted will bear heavily against the defendant." However, DeShong admitted on cross-examination that he disliked Parker and had remarked publicly that he ought to be hanged—though he denied saying that he desired to help accomplish it. Rather, he merely said that should this happy event occur, he would be certain not to miss it. DeShong asserted that he and Wills had not stolen the Parker dog; it was a friendly sort that followed them even after they tried to make it return home. It was Wills's idea to take the knives, and neither boy had any intention of ever returning to the farm. He admitted firing a Colt pistol twice at their pursuers. He heard Parker's fatal shot but did not see it. Contrary to all previously published reports, DeShong said he and Wills had not quarreled with Parker over their pay, or rather the lack of it; they just felt the urge to wander, and Wills took the corn knives in lieu of pay for work they had already done.

Witness James Ewing solved the mystery of where Parker went directly after shooting Wills. He had gone to Ewing's house, where, according to the witness, Parker asked, "Are you my friend?"

"I am."

"Will you go up the pike with me tomorrow morning?"

"Why?

"I shot a man."

"Did you kill him?"

"Yes, dead as hell. He took my dog and corn knife."

The significant part of the dialogue, according to the prosecution, was what Parker *didn't* say. He did not claim the shooting was accidental.

A new witness, R.M. Tipton, saw neither Wills waving his hat nor Parker's horse swerving.

April 3 saw the continuance of what one newspaper called "one of the most interesting murder trials ever had in central Kentucky." Judge George W.C. Graves testified that he had sold Parker the horse he was riding when the unpleasantness occurred and that the mare had "the habit of shying at meeting persons in the road." She had almost thrown Graves several times and once had actually tossed the otherwise dignified judge into the road.

Michael Sullivan discussed his adventure of sitting overnight with Wills's body, as it was stored in a spring wagon in a shed, but he had nothing to add to the store of knowledge on the case except that no one tampered with the corpse.

R. Benjamin Graves, a witness who had already been heard from, testified that only a few minutes after the shooting, Parker told him and his wife that Wills spooked the mare with a sudden movement, causing the tragic accident. Mrs. Graves corroborated her husband when she spoke in the afternoon session.

The prosecution objected when a diagram showing the exact locations of witnesses, landmarks and the death spot was produced for the jury, since it was labeled "the spot where the accident occurred." They argued that the draftsman was prejudiced in favor of the defense's theory and was trying to influence the jury. The court ruled that the diagram was admissible if the offending words were erased.

William Cromwell and John T. Wood swore that they had visited the scene of the crime (or mishap—take your pick); performed experiments, such as shouting, speaking in tones of varying volume and firing pistols; and determined that the prosecution witnesses could not have seen or heard what they claimed. Six other men on rebuttal said they had gone to the site, performed similar tests and decided that the witnesses *could* have seen and heard what they claimed—so there. Again, take your pick.

***

The arguments ended, and the jury retired on the evening of April 3. They had quite a task before them. A contemporary reporter noted the *Rashomon*-style confusion they faced:

> [Consider] *the many contradictions between witnesses on the same side, and the inconsistency of many of their statements with others made by themselves, and it will become almost impossible to attach any credence to a general impression formed from all the evidence in the case.…And so it is with almost all the testimony in the case; it is so contradicted, directly or indirectly by other evidence, that no clear idea of its weight can be had.*

Of all the witnesses, Montgomery Parker Jr. was closest to the action and in the best position to tell what actually happened, but DeShong swore that Parker could not have seen all he that he claimed from his vantage point. Compounding the uncertainty, a man named Frank Storms said DeShong was incorrect.

To make the jury's lot even harder, April 4 was the final day of the court term, and the members were under pressure to reach a verdict by midnight, or they would be discharged and the case delayed until the next session. Perhaps that is why, just half an hour before midnight, the jury announced they were hopelessly deadlocked and were dismissed. Their final vote was two for murder, five for manslaughter and five for acquittal. Considering all the confusion and contradiction, dismissal was the proper decision.

Montgomery Parker was free under a $15,000 bond until the next court session began. On April 17, he received an anonymous threatening note telling him lynchers would pay a call on April 30. Since mobs usually didn't inform their victims in advance of their intentions, no one was surprised when the date came and went without incident.

The circuit court reconvened for a special session to try Parker on February 2, 1875. Rumor held that he had fled the country, but he turned up at the courthouse right on time. Some bungling clerk improperly docketed the case, so it was delayed until early April, exactly a year after the first trial. Interestingly, Clifton Crim, who had undergone a bout of temporary insanity the last time around and therefore hadn't made it to court for a few days, went crazy again with impeccable—some might say suspicious—timing. The case ended again with a hung jury.

The third go-around began on May 17, but the indictment was dismissed after one of the grand jurors was disqualified. On May 26, news came that there had been a change of venue to Woodford County. And then—nothing! The press had nothing more to say about the case. Was it dismissed? Was Parker acquitted? A stone-cold clue can be found, perhaps, in Lexington Cemetery, where Parker's grave marker bears the death year 1877. Maybe the trial was delayed again and Parker died before it recommenced, so cheated earthly justice—*if* he committed intentional murder, not accidental manslaughter. A vigorously shaken Magic 8 Ball's guess is as good as anyone's.

20

THE VERY AIR ABOUNDS IN KINGS

Few murders were ever committed under such unpleasant circumstances. In mid-February 1899, the nation was blasted with a freakish cold snap, and to make matters worse, there was a coal shortage. Kentucky suffered under the lowest temperatures ever recorded in the state up to that time. If you were lucky, the thermometer measured merely 10 degrees below zero; if unlucky, it showed a temperature of -42 degrees. And should the wind blow—ah, God help you then!

It was -20 degrees in Lexington on February 11, when twenty-one-year-old John Henry Beckers McNamara, nicknamed "King" for reasons that do not appear in the record, shot Jacob Spears Keller twice with a revolver on Main Street, in front of the courthouse. The wounded man was rushed to St. Joseph's Hospital, and McNamara was arrested. The shooter came from a prominent family, "a power in local politics," as the earliest news accounts stated.

Interestingly, the *Mt. Sterling Sentinel-Democrat* noted that McNamara carried a gun despite Kentucky's concealed weapons law that made it a felony. The newspaper asserted, foreshadowing modern pro-gun arguments, that the counterproductive law ensured only that law-abiding citizens went unarmed and were thus easy prey for the less scrupulous.

"King" was released on bond within an hour of the shooting, probably only because Keller wasn't dead yet, but let's not forget those political connections. The victim, a thirty-seven-year-old cashier at the Cincinnati Southern freight office, died on February 13, leaving behind a wife and family.

McNamara was rearrested, this time for murder. He was bailed out again for $1,000, an amount far too low considering the gravity of his offense, according to Honorable John T. Shelby. McNamara shafted his bondsmen and fled the city before nightfall. By shooting a man and vanishing, King—let's dispense with those quotation marks—strained the limits of his family's political popularity. Governor Bradley offered a reward of $150 for his capture (the modern equivalent is almost $6,000), which was increased to $300 on February 20. On the same day, members of every woman's club in the city met at Mrs. Robert A. Thornton's house to plan a mass meeting that was to be held at Merrick Lodge the next day. Their object was to help the authorities catch McNamara.

"King" McNamara. *Louisville Courier-Journal*, March 1, 1899. *Courtesy of the* Louisville Courier-Journal.

King was gone, but a special jury convened to try him in absentia on February 21. Judge Watts Parker lamented that "he was forced almost daily to see the ends of justice defeated." He blamed it on wimpy juries. Said a reporter: "He had seen murderers covered with guilt taken from the courtroom amidst the applause of their friends when they should have been borne to the gallows instead." Parker added with judicial common sense that criminals turned loose on society thanks to misplaced mercy were likely to claim more lives: "He said the office of a juror was a responsible position; that the blood of succeeding victims was on the hands of the jury acquitting the guilty murderer; that the punishing of the criminal for the first offense would have saved the life of the second victim." Additionally, the judge made a few remarks about how wealth and connections "figured too largely in meting out justice." The special jury took the hint and indicted McNamara.

On the same day, frostbitten citizens, warmed only by their own anger, met primarily to raise an even larger reward for King's capture. Their secondary reason for meeting was to show Lexington's criminals that law-abiding citizens were sick of their shenanigans and would tolerate them no more. (Apparently, the city was quite the hotbed of crime in 1899. At the meeting, citizen Robert A. Thompson said Lexington's toleration of evildoing had become a national joke: "The name of Lexington was a hiss and a by-word all over the land.") Another attendee, Judge Jere Morton, counseled moderation and caution and suggested the meeting adopt no resolutions, just the sort of wussiness the assembly was formed to condemn. He was overruled by a majority of votes. In the end, the committee unanimously adopted several resolutions. One urged citizens to contribute to a reward for King's capture and asked the governor to increase the state's reward. That meant there would be two bounties for McNamara's apprehension, one provided by the government and the other provided by private citizens.

Governor Bradley obligingly increased the state's reward to the $500 maximum, the fiscal court added $500 more and Lexingtonians scraped up an additional $1,000, making the total $2,000. (The modern equivalent is almost $76,000.) With that kind of money in 1899, you could have purchased a sumptuous, fully furnished new house with state-of-the-art technology, such as electric lights and indoor plumbing, while your envious neighbors had to make do with oil lamps and the fragrant, cholera-breeding outhouse. This amount of money meant, of course, that people who were "powerful hongry" for the payment thought they had seen King everywhere in the continental United States.

For example, police officers in Kankakee, Illinois, believed David Blackwell, a consumptive in their jail for shooting a railway watchman on February 17, was McNamara traveling incognito. Blackwell insisted that he was a Spanish-American War veteran whose home was located in Shelby, Indiana. He was correct.

Some theorized that King had not traveled far at all and was really hiding in Lexington, just waiting for the reward on his hide to become larger. Then the rascal would allow a friend to turn him in and collect the money, so the conspirator could use it to hire a lawyer to get King off—in effect, forcing citizens to use their own reward to set him free. This fiendishly clever ruse never came to pass.

J.C. Chester, aka Chester Allen, was arrested in New Orleans on March 11, 1899. Police there had received a circular describing King, whose appearance tallied "very closely with Chester's description, particularly in respect to stature, color of hair, and a scar under the left eye." But it was not King.

August 1901 brought the news that King McNamara had certainly been found at last, not far from Seattle, Washington. "Secret steps are being taken to secure his arrest and return," assured the *Louisville Courier-Journal*, but one wonders how secret the plan could have been after being announced in a newspaper story. This man, whomever he was, also was not King.

A few days later, a Lexington policeman, Samuel T. Weeks, spread a rumor that the fugitive was in Colorado. Weeks was arrested for lunacy on August 19.

Sacramento police nabbed Frank Rogers on September 16 after he was mistaken for the missing King. California officials sent Rogers's picture to Lexington police, who sadly wired back that the arrestee didn't even resemble McNamara.

But then, On February 5, 1911, a week short of the murder's anniversary, a man marched into New York City's West Thirtieth Street police station and said, "My name is King McNamara. I killed a man in Lexington, Kentucky, on February 18, 1897. Arrest me and send me back." He added that he was currently a fireman and thirty-one years old. Obsessive-compulsive readers will have noticed already that the murder really occurred on February 11, 1899, and that, in February 1911, McNamara should have been thirty-three, not thirty-one. Do you hear alarm bells?

The next day, the prisoner told the judge that after shooting his victim ("I don't know his name"), he jumped on a passing train and went to New Orleans and then to San Francisco, where he joined a circus and had since been traveling the nation, presumably basking in glory with equestrians, prodigies and rat-eating geeks. The prisoner explained that he didn't feel a whit sorry for the man he killed, whoever he was, but thought he had been on the run long enough and that if he stood trial, he would be acquitted on grounds of self-defense. Being a fugitive was just too inconvenient. A question that troubled many people surfaced: Since King had turned *himself* in, what was going to happen to that $2,000 reward, which, in part, had been collecting dust in a Lexington bank vault for many years?

Two Fayette County deputy sheriffs, C.H. "Kit" Wilkerson and C.L. Wilson, traveled to New York to bring McNamara to Kentucky. Many were not convinced that the prisoner was actually King, including King's brothers (the surviving ones, that is), one of whom said to a reporter, "King is not in that part of the country and has not been there for years to my knowledge." He added, untroubled that he could be charged with aiding and abetting a fugitive murderer, "We know where he is, of course, and hear from him all the time.…He has a good job, is making money, is behaving himself, is a good citizen, and prospering." He showed the reporter a snazzy pocket watch that he claimed was a Christmas gift from the missing King and added that King would have sent his family a telegram if he had surrendered.

It seemed the police had their man at last, especially after Deputy Sheriffs Wilkerson and Wilson, who had known McNamara, positively identified him. Nevertheless, there was so much skepticism that, even as the deputies were returning to Lexington with their captive, many citizens had a betting pool over whether the arrestee really was King. It was said that at least $1,000 had been wagered, and one of the anti-McNamara bettors was former Judge Frank Bullock. Sheriff Dan Scott staked $300 on the pro-McNamara side. On February 10, a crowd of at least five hundred awaited the train's arrival, despite the earliness of the hour. Howls of laughter and jeers, such as "That ain't King!" and "I thought you had McNamara!" greeted the lawmen when they stepped out with yet another imposter. A reporter who had a swell time rubbing salt in the deputies' wounds started his article with, "Lexington was in a broad grin and a titter tonight." Many unkindly disposed persons noted that the man under arrest didn't remotely resemble McNamara, even factoring in twelve years of aging. When asked why he lied, the fraud answered lamely, "I *thought* I was McNamara." He had murdered nothing but the truth.

Ironically, even if the prisoner had been the authentic King McNamara, none of the original government reward money from 1899 would have been paid, since Governor Willson had canceled all outstanding rewards for criminals when his term began on January 1, 1910.

The Man Who Would Be King was really John "Soldier" Vialls, a former prizefighter and one-time Lexington resident, which explained his convincing knowledge of the city's minutiae and everyday life. However, he knew little about the McNamara family. He could not locate their house, did not know where King had gone to school (St. Paul's Academy) and, when detectives asked the alleged McNamara how many sisters he had and what their names were, he replied with a splendid non sequitur: "My head hurts."

In the days before people were entertained by Netflix and YouTube, anyone who achieved some measure of notoriety was sure to receive an offer to appear on the stage; it was the same for Vialls, whose claim to fame might seem rather paltry. On February 11, the famous New York Klaw and Erlanger vaudeville circuit offered him $100 (in modern currency, almost $3,300) per week to exhibit himself as the man who fooled law enforcement by pretending to be an uncaught murderer. Lexington's Police Chief Reagan thought seriously of quitting his job and becoming Vialls's manager, and he announced that $100 weekly wasn't *nearly* enough pay for his putative client—and if the show business professionals balked, he would exhibit Vialls himself at a dime a head. The sudden fame got to Vialls, too. He was noticeably snobbish to his fellow cellmates except for a humble, elderly chicken thief with whom he struck up a friendship.

Vialls and McNamara. Why—they are veritable twins! *Louisville Courier-Journal*, February 12, 1911. *Courtesy of the* Louisville Courier-Journal.

Vialls was faking his dissociative fugue state but "remembered" his true identity quickly enough after receiving the offer of easy vaudeville riches. After all, to sign a legally binding contract, he had to know who he really was! On February 12, he confessed. He had known McNamara when they were kids and remembered Keller's murder; he claimed that confessing to the crime just seemed the thing to do. The idea came to him when he was drunk, and he was amazed that those stupid New York police had believed him. He said they wouldn't give him a chance to explain himself (he forgot to mention that he had signed papers officially swearing he was King McNamara of good old Kentucky); he really didn't want to return to Lexington anyway, so now he sure would like to go back to New York. Others thought his real motive was a free ride home to Lexington.

The *Courier-Journal* ran an editorial called "Degraders of the Stage" on February 13, which decried vaudeville for putting any infamous person onstage and noted that such exhibitions often failed: "The public must at least be amused. It is not amused for a great while by satisfying its curiosity as to the appearance of a man or woman who has figured in the headlines, but who has no capacity as an entertainer." Perhaps Vialls intended to burnish his act by reciting poetry or doing the latest dance sensation, the foxtrot. Klaw and Erlanger must have had second thoughts, since there is no record of Vialls appearing onstage even once, let alone becoming the next matinée idol, but at least the failure prevented a spate of opportunists hoping to ride the gravy train by falsely assuming a murderer's identity.

In fact, Vialls's little stunt landed him in a legal predicament. On February 13, a warrant was sworn out for him, charging him with falsely impersonating King McNamara and accepting railroad fare for a fancy Pullman car and free meals during his trip from New York with the deputies. These were felonies, so if he was found guilty, he would be penitentiary bound. Vialls protested that he had meant no harm and blamed everything on that Bowery rotgut he drank. He was released on February 25, after the judge ruled that since his offenses were committed before he crossed the border into Kentucky, the state had no jurisdiction. New York pressed no charges and seemed rather glad to be rid of Vialls.

Though stage glory was but an ephemeral dream, Vialls's sudden fame rejuvenated his Lexington boxing career. And the fiasco yielded some benefits for justice. Long-forgotten King McNamara was back in the news, renewing an eagle-eyed public's eagerness for his capture, especially after it was realized that while Governor Willson had canceled the *government's* reward money, the $1,000 bounty offered by private citizens was still in effect. In fact, it had been collecting 3 percent interest since 1899 and was said to now be closer to $1,500. Also, Sheriff Scott was so angered by the public humiliation of his deputies that he vowed he would find McNamara if it was the last thing he ever did. Then there was the fact that the fugitive's brothers foolhardily had revealed that he was still alive somewhere.

While all these adventures in mistaken identity were going on, other members of McNamara's politically prominent family tangled with the law, to make a tepid understatement. Indeed, they made the later Kennedys of Massachusetts look like pikers. The father of the family, Matthew "Red Mack" McNamara, made his fortune by operating a popular saloon at the corner of Main and Spring Streets; he got in trouble long before the Keller murder by stabbing a railroad conductor to death in a fight. Red Mack died on June 29, 1887.

On February 23, 1899, only a few days after King shot Keller, King's brother William J., nicknamed "Jady"—and a magistrate at that—was arrested and indicted on six charges: three for carrying concealed weapons, one for assaulting Nick Ryan, one for assaulting Police Captain A.J.

Ferra and one for shooting and wounding a Black soldier named George Knickerbocker (or it might have been Ferdinand Caldwell; accounts differ, which is understandable considering the striking similarity between the two names). The authorities, probably embarrassed at the smooth ease with which King made bond twice and then escaped, set his brother's bail at $2,200 total. William was tried in circuit court on March 7 and walked out after the jury couldn't reach a verdict. But his freedom was temporary; the next day, the jury agreed, and McNamara was sentenced to three years in state prison. His attorneys made a motion for a new trial, but it was overruled on March 31. They need not have bothered, since he was pardoned in December, a move that some thought reeked of political string-pulling. But at least he had to stay in jail until he paid $450 in fines. On August 16, 1901, William was killed in a fight with John Meager in J.W. Darby's saloon.

Another brother, Thomas (uniquely to this story, he was *not* nicknamed), went to jail on February 25, 1899, for contempt of court after he refused to tell the grand jury what he knew about his missing brother's whereabouts. Everyone fully expected him to remain in jail until further notice, but he was released without official comment at noon on February 28. Eventually, he imitated his brother John by killing a man and fleeing the city. He returned, went on trial and was acquitted. Thomas, the owner of a saloon at 442 West Main Street and a Democratic Party leader, was shot to death in Blanche Patterson's brothel by Robert McNamee on March 23, 1910. He died at St. Joseph's Hospital, the same place where King's victim had died.

Another brother, Edward Francis, age about forty-three, "of a quiet and peaceable disposition" and one of the last of the McNamaras, shot himself in the head on March 7, 1914, after a long illness. He didn't expire until March 11. However, since the coroner said Edward sported *four* bullets in his head, we might take the suicide verdict with a grain of salt.

But now we must return to John "King" McNamara; the main character in our drama has been offstage too long. In March 1912, Lexington's Sheriff Scott, acting on a tip from a Louisville woman, traveled to that city. He didn't find McNamara but left Detective James Steward (or Stewart), formerly of Omaha, Nebraska, in charge of the manhunt.

On June 13, Steward sent a telegram to Sheriff Scott, telling him their quarry had been positively identified. Scott and two deputies immediately left for Louisville and checked into the Tyler Hotel. The next morning, Steward called Scott to inform him that the suspect was on the way to the Seelbach Hotel (now the Seelbach Hilton). Scott, Steward and their deputies arrived there just in time to see their man walking through the ladies' entrance—a sign, perhaps, that he suspected something was up and was trying to sneak into the building. The officers pounced as he rang for an elevator.

Sheriff Scott, it will be remembered, had lost a cool $300 the year before when he wagered that the man his deputies were bringing from New York was King McNamara, so it must have given him special satisfaction when he slipped the handcuffs on the genuine King, who had lived in Louisville since 1908 under the name Dr. James Baker. Since 1910, he had been a veterinary assistant to Dr. John T. Chawk. "Baker" numbered some of Louisville's most prominent citizens as his acquaintances and customers, and their astonishment at finding that he was really the long-sought McNamara bordered on comedy. Dr. Chawk's words drip with a certain irony: "Everybody liked him. He was kind, generous, and gentlemanly. I told him he was too soft-hearted to be a veterinarian. He couldn't stand the sight of blood. He apparently couldn't bear to see anybody suffer.... He was just as good an employee as a man would want. I never dreamed of any dark past."

The sheriff took King back to his home city immediately. The captive lamented, "Thank God my poor old mother is dead!" Once in jail, he did not deny his identity. Major changes had taken place in the family's fortunes in the twelve years since 1899; as a reporter summarized, "Two of his brothers have been killed since McNamara fled and the family, which was once wealthy and a strong power in politics, have, through the misconduct of the brothers, lost much of both fortune and influence, though they still have considerable property and have some strong political connections."

Now that King was caught, a loose end had to be tied: Who would get that $1,500 reward? The press said that Sheriff Scott was first tipped off to McNamara's presence in Louisville by a woman. She was unmasked as the "pretty and intelligent" Detective Bettie Foss of Chicago. She had made the acquaintance of "Dr. James Baker" and charmed him until he let his guard down and revealed that he was really McNamara. He told her that he lived in Louisville most of the time while on the run, that he had attended the Lexington funerals of his mother and brothers with impunity and that he had never been arrested because he had influence with the police departments of Lexington and Louisville. The police in both cities denied McNamara's last boast. Louisville's Night Chief of Police Ridge pointed out that letting McNamara slide would have meant not collecting the reward. Many officials probably thought McNamara had been talking big to impress cute young Bettie Foss. The prisoner's family finally fessed up that he had hidden in

Arizona and Montana several years before heading back to Kentucky after the heat was off.

On a couple of points, Foss was undoubtedly correct. She knew where the fugitive lived. Also, she explained how McNamara had escaped detection for so long, even while living in his home state. One of his chief identifying marks was a large scar on his left temple from a childhood accident. But while on the lam, he bragged to her, he had hired a surgeon to cut a piece of skin off his right arm and graft it over the scar. The young detective told Sheriff Scott that if he inspected McNamara's arm, he would see where the skin was removed. McNamara refused to discuss Bettie Foss with reporters, perhaps because he was embarrassed that he had been caught by a woman detective. The Second National Bank was slow to give her the reward, and on June 20, her Chicago attorney, the majestically named A. Hale Vollintine, filed a claim for it.

Another competitor for the big bucks was Detective James Steward, who kept watch on McNamara when Sheriff Scott was absent from Louisville. Others argued that Scott should have the reward, since it was promised "for the arrest and delivery of McNamara to the jailer of Fayette County," and the sheriff was the person who fit that bill. On the other hand, Scott had promised to give the money—all of it—to Foss for her help. A disappointment for all claimants was that the payout was actually $200, not $1,500 as reported, and little explanation for the incredible shrinking reward was forthcoming. Ex-Sheriff Scott himself filed a suit for the cash as late as March 1914. There is no record that anyone got so much as a shiny new nickel of the reward.

Our tale began with extreme temperatures, and it closes with the same—but in the opposite direction on the thermometer. A nationwide heat wave was underway when McNamara's trial began on July 8, 1912. The courtroom was "packed to suffocation," and no doubt, the balmy weather made it seem worse. Long-dead victim Jacob Keller's brother John Esten and two sisters, Lucy and Helen, were undaunted by the heat and attended every court session.

King McNamara pleaded not guilty. The defense refused to reveal their strategy for saving his hide, but when they finally did, there were no surprises. His attorneys, John R. Riley, Samuel U. Wilson and Wallace Muir, could hardly deny that their client had murdered Keller, so they offered what we now call a "diminished capacity" defense: he was drunk as a spider monkey at the time and didn't know what he was doing. There was no malice aforethought! (They didn't mention that even if there was no malice *before* the crime, there certainly was *during* it, but that might have been counterproductive to McNamara's interests.) They also brought in a parade of witnesses, including former Mayor John Skain and former Sheriff Waller Rodes, who testified to the defendant's sterling character before and after February 11, 1899, therefore he must not be judged based solely on his behavior on that uncharacteristic day: "[He] has reformed and would now become a useful and respected citizen." I call this the "everyone has a bad day sometimes" argument. Others bluntly and contrarily characterized McNamara as "the town bully."

McNamara testified on July 10. The courtroom was so packed, people had to be turned away. "Soldier" Vialls would have loved to draw such a crowd had that vaudeville contract worked out. King refused to discuss exactly how or where he spent his thirteen years in hiding but admitted that he had returned to Lexington, despite being a wanted man. He wouldn't say how often he had returned. He had been slightly crazy ever since that childhood head injury that caused the scar on his temple. Also, he had been drunk for a month. And Keller had made what he interpreted to be a threatening gesture, so he shot in self-defense.

The case went to the jury on July 11. Before they retired to deliberate, Judge Samuel Wilson gave dubious instructions to the jury: "In order for the Commonwealth to make out a case of murder, it must not only show that McNamara shot and killed Keller, but it must show that the shooting was done with malice aforethought, which it will not be able to do because neither McNamara nor Keller knew each other." What, so it isn't possible to feel malicious toward a total stranger? However, the judge's argument convinced the jury—or maybe they thought King's admitted drunkenness was a reasonable excuse, or perhaps they thought the killing was done in self-defense. After twenty-three hours' deliberation, they found McNamara guilty only of manslaughter. He was sentenced to a laughable five years in prison. His attorneys did not appeal, nor did McNamara ask them to. Likely, they all secretly felt he had gotten off easy and didn't want to push their luck with a second trial. "The murderer who succeeds in securing delay gains an advantage," editorialized the *Courier-Journal*.

McNamara had lived a free and easy existence for thirteen years after his crime; was found guilty not of murder but of a lesser charge; his sentence called for imprisonment "at labor"—not the usual phrase "at *hard* labor"—which some interpreted to mean he would get a cushy desk job. Surely enough, he got one in the prison hospital. And there was a minor controversy when he was given a car ride to Frankfort Penitentiary while eight other Lexington prisoners who were sentenced at the same time had to go by train.

McNamara wound up serving far less than three years of his already generous five-year sentence. He was paroled on December 11, 1914. As both Mel Brooks and Tom Petty have observed, it's good to be King. His defense team may have been correct that he had been reformed; it appears he got into no more trouble—such as shooting an unarmed man and fleeing the state—for the rest of his life. He moved back to Louisville and died in the Jefferson Home for the Aged and Infirm on April 27, 1949, and was buried in Calvary Cemetery. At the time of his death, he was a sanitation department worker.

So, why *did* King McNamara shoot Keller on that long-ago, sub-zero day in 1899, anyway? Keller had demanded an apology after McNamara stepped on his heels, and King, resenting the impudence, said, "Get off the earth." And then he shot him. So, at least he didn't murder Keller for any *stupid* reason.

21

POET AND POISONER

James Hilary Mulligan was born in Lexington on November 21, 1844. He got his law degree from Transylvania University in 1869 and became a noted judge. He was a member of the Kentucky House of Representatives from 1881 to 1888 and was state senator from 1890 to 1891. He also wrote light verse, and one of his productions, "In Kentucky," created such a sensation that it is still one of the most famous poems ever written about the state, ranking right up there with Stephen Foster's "My Old Kentucky Home" and Theodore O'Hara's "Bivouac of the Dead." Had he copyrighted it, contemporaries noted, he would have made a fortune. A columnist once said in 1915, "It has been parodied a thousand times, reproduced in almost every newspaper in English and more than a million souvenir postal cards have been sold with the verses printed upon them." It's sort of like those ubiquitous modern Baby Yodas, but you can bet those are copyrighted. The final verse is by far the most famous:

The song birds are the sweetest,
In Kentucky;
The thoroughbreds the fleetest,
In Kentucky;
Mountains tower proudest,
Thunder peals the loudest,
The landscape is the grandest—
And politics—the damndest,
In Kentucky.

This was considered quite naughty at the time. Two years after the poem was published, something naughtier occurred in Mulligan's Maxwell Place home that threatened to surpass the poem's fame and perhaps end the lives of the judge and his family.

Judge Mulligan. *Louisville Courier-Journal*, July 2, 1915. *Courtesy of the* Louisville Courier-Journal.

On September 24, 1904, Judge Mulligan was not present, but the rest of his family sat in the dining room at lunchtime to enjoy the delights of baked salmon with salad. Those in the home included the judge's second wife, Genevieve, and their four children: Denis, Kathleen, Marion and Willoughby, the baby of the family. Before anyone could take a bite, their noticeably nervous Black employee Louis (or Lewis) Mitchell, called Denis out of the room.

"Don't eat the fish! It's poisoned!" he said.

Denis wasted no time telling the others to avoid the lunch if they valued their lives. When the judge was apprised, he called for detectives. Of course, they asked Mitchell how he knew the meal was tainted. "One of the Mulligan relatives paid me to poison the fish," he confessed. Mrs. Mulligan had saved him from going to the penitentiary once, and now, he wanted to return the favor. Police arrested Mitchell, who was the family's carriage driver, cow milker and handyman.

Detectives took the salmon to Professor Alfred Peter of the Chemistry Department at State University (to become the University of Kentucky twelve years later). The verdict: the food was lousy with powdered arsenic. It contained more than twelve grains, sufficient to kill several people. Who could have ordered Mitchell to put it there? It was well known that three of the four children who were had by Mulligan's his first wife, Mary, who died in 1876, did not get along with Genevieve or her offspring. These three were Alice, married to P.H. Molloy, Fayette County coroner; James Jr., who lived in Chicago; and Mary (nicknamed Mollie), who had just married army Corporal Frank Stevenson a few days before the attempted poisoning after a courtship of only two weeks. The fourth—and the only one on good terms with his stepmother—was thirty-five-year-old Louis, who still lived in Lexington and was an assistant physician at the Eastern Asylum for the Insane.

The judge's father, Dennis (spelled differently than the judge's son Denis), had died in 1900, followed by Mulligan's mother, Ellen, earlier in 1904. Her will could not be found, so Judge Mulligan, as the only heir, was about to inherit a considerable fortune, estimated at between $100,000 and $150,000, plus property in Lexington, Kansas and Illinois. It also meant that the judge could split the money with his children by his second wife, Genevieve, and rumor held that his children by Mary were displeased at the prospect of being forced to share a watered-down inheritance with their half-siblings. The leading story among rumormongers was that one of Mary's jealous children wanted to poison the family, and it seemed confirmed when Louis Mitchell said the motive of the still-unnamed person who hired him was to gain control of the legacy.

It should have been easy to narrow the list of suspects, but while he was in jail, Louis told his story officially, with added contradictory and bizarre details. At 5:30 a.m. on September 24, he had arrived at the Mulligan house to work. He took the salmon, which had been prepared the day before by cook Emma Morton, out of the icebox. He was about to help himself to a spoonful when he saw white powder on it. He thought it was quinine, a drug then used to treat malaria, and decided he didn't want a bite after all. Mitchell's story didn't make much sense in several respects. If a Mulligan relative paid him to poison the lunch, then he should have known darn well the powder wasn't quinine, because he would have been the person who put it there. He even drew Emma's attention to the strange substance but then told her to keep quiet about it—or so Emma told police: "He also said that a relative of Judge Mulligan had said to him that there would be a court scrap and that he would have his revenge." (Note that the relative was a "he.") Emma also said that Louis told her he would be getting money soon and could leave the city. After Louis supposedly revealed the entire evil plot to Emma, he served the fish, decided he didn't want to be a killer-for-hire after all and alerted Denis just as he was about to partake. In a second confession Mitchell made in the afternoon, he told police an additional weird story, which no one believed, about seeing a figure dressed all in black in the yard the night before, unmistakably a woman trying to disguise herself as a man. Mitchell

Dennis (not Denis) Mulligan. *Louisville Courier-Journal*, September 29, 1904. *Courtesy of the* Louisville Courier-Journal.

also claimed that when he entered the kitchen early Saturday morning, a masked man pointed a gun at him and told him to go to the barn. Mitchell said he did as he was bidden, and when he returned, the man was gone. This character must have wanted Louis to vacate the kitchen so he could taint the fish, but contrarily, Louis also said someone paid him to do it.

The police also arrested the cook Emma, since she had easy access to the food. She protested her innocence. The Mulligans, who had employed her for years, believed her, and she was released. She went right back to work in the kitchen, eloquent proof that the family trusted her.

When the judge first called in Chief of Detectives J.W. Marshall, he told him it was a "family affair" and requested that it be kept out of the newspapers. Plainly, Mulligan, too, suspected the would-be killer was a member of his family.

Mitchell underwent another examination on the morning of September 26, and this time, he named names. The man who hired him was James Mulligan Jr., who was in town for his sister's wedding, and he was paid $100. Mitchell claimed that the primary target was his stepmother "Miss Jennie" (Genevieve), but if he killed anyone else as collateral damage, why, that was fine with James Jr.

Judge Mulligan didn't believe Mitchell's story (or rather, stories), and James Jr. hotly denied them all—by telephone, since he had returned to Chicago after the wedding. He came back to Lexington on September 27 to clear his name and took a room at the Phoenix Hotel. The next day, Genevieve Mulligan hired guards to watch their Maxwell Place house. Did she fear that James—or someone else—would try again?

The public loves a good mystery, and Lexington was abuzz with pet theories. Some believed Louis Mitchell told the truth about James Jr.'s attempt to kill his stepmother and half-siblings. Others thought Louis, who garnished his story with such dubious details, was the real culprit, though no one could understand why he would want to murder the woman whose influence kept him out of prison years before. A third faction held that Mitchell's confession was mostly true, but he was lying about the identity of the villain who had bribed him. Rumor held that the Mulligans' powerful friends were trying to scotch the investigation before the shocking "real truth" was discovered. That may not have been true, but it was a fact that the city's detectives stopped investigating after Mitchell's confession. Others said that the only way to clear any suspected family member (they meant James Jr.) was to allow the case to be investigated fully and go to the grand jury. Judge Mulligan said that if the evidence pointed to his son, he would allow

The silver dish that held the poisoned salmon. Judge Mulligan said the handles reminded him of coffin handles. *Lexington Herald*, September 25, 1904. *Courtesy of the* Lexington Herald-Leader.

justice to take its course and would not drop the charges. Possibly tellingly, while James Jr. was staying at the hotel, no members of his family came to visit—not even his father, though James asked him twice—except his sister Alice Molloy. The younger James hired a Chicago detective, L.P. Colleran, to come to Lexington and do independent snooping.

Louis Mitchell's examining trial began on October 7. It was a pageant of embarrassments for the Mulligans, as it forced them, under oath, to take the family's skeletons out of the closet and give them a good public polishing. The judge, Genevieve and Denis Mulligan testified about the lack of harmony between the four older children and the four younger ones. Denis also spoke of Mitchell's strange behavior just before serving the salmon, which suggested he was nervous about some imminent event.

Genevieve said her relations with James Jr. were "always kind and affectionate." But she also related a disturbing incident from three years before, in which James said that he intended to drown himself in Chicago on his next birthday, but before he did, he said he would "commit a crime that would startle the world," which would involve removing from this world three other persons whom he did not name. Since James neither died by suicide nor indulged in a murder spree, the family evidently dismissed his vow as big talk. (When asked about it in court, he said he didn't remember saying such an extravagant thing.)

Judge Mulligan admitted under oath that his relations with his daughter Mary (Mollie) were strained, starting three years before, when he forbade her from going on an excursion to Mammoth Cave with some boys he disapproved of. The argument was serious enough that she moved in with her married sister, Alice. James Jr.'s formerly pleasant association with his family turned sour afterward. Judge Mulligan had also objected to Mary's recent marriage to Frank Stevenson—so much that he refused to give her money to buy wedding clothes. Mulligan complained that he barely had even met the groom, and besides, he was *merely* a corporal. Adding to the family's mortification, letters from James Jr. to his father and stepmother, in which he excoriated both bitterly, were read aloud.

Emma Morton retold the story of Mitchell's foreknowledge that the lunch was poisoned. She didn't believe him until the chemistry professor corroborated it.

James Jr. confirmed earlier testimony that he had gotten along harmoniously with his family until his sister Mary left the house. A reporter summarized, "Mollie said to him that home had been made unbearable to her and that she could not stay there any longer." He admitted that his stepmother had always been kind to him and said the reason for his grudge was not being shafted out of part of his inheritance but rather what he considered Mary's shabby treatment.

On October 8, Louis Mitchell's attorney James Denny said his client ought to be acquitted; not only that, but Judge Mulligan should also be grateful that Mitchell's quick actions and guilty conscience saved his family from being poisoned. Denny alleged that James Jr. *and* Genevieve Mulligan poisoned the salmon. The only basis for his accusation seemed to be gossip that blamed them both; they had been "accused at the bar of public sentiment," he said, a poor legal standard indeed. Prosecutor Jere Morton called this "a base slander on the name of fair womanhood"—after all, she had been "born and educated a lady"—which, like Denny's charge, also seems an appeal to the emotions rather than reason or evidence. This was followed by long, lovely, fawning, slightly nauseating tributes to Mrs. Mulligan by Morton and attorney John R. Allen.

Dr. Louis Mulligan testified that he had lived at home until he got that great job as an assistant physician at the insane asylum, and he attested that he had never seen his stepmother show any favoritism to her natural children. He admitted that his sisters, Mary and Alice, hadn't visited home in a long time but implied that was their father's fault, not Genevieve's. Magistrate Oldham ruled that servant Louis Mitchell would have to face the grand jury in a trial for attempted murder. The grand jury's investigation continued.

Now that the suggestion of Mrs. Mulligan's being the potential murderer had been publicly raised in court, Judge Mulligan—once eager to keep the story out of the papers and the courtroom—indignantly demanded that every lead be followed to its end, as he wanted to clear Genevieve's name: "For my wife and in her name, I defy and invite the investigation of any and all the detectives." He didn't really mean it, though. The next day, October 11, he blew his stack when another Chicago detective, W.E. Burke, watched his son Denis in the courthouse. He promised nosy detectives a lingering death and blistered James Jr.'s hide while he was at it.

"I have stood the slander from this recreant sot of a son as long as I can," he thundered. "And from now on, the scabbard is off, and it is war to the knife. I give warning to all, be they snide lawyers [a shout-out to James Denny] or detectives, that if they invent any slander on my wife or any member of my family, I will avenge it with [my] life's blood, and if I am killed in the attempt to protect the good name of my wife, I will leave others behind to avenge my death." It's not every day you get bodily threatened by a judge and poet who also called for a vendetta in the event of his death, and the detectives kept their theories quiet after this tirade. In fact, the two Chicago sleuths didn't even appear at the courthouse the next day.

Two major developments came on October 13: James Mulligan Jr. was exonerated, but Louis Mitchell was indicted. (Mrs. Mulligan's name wasn't even mentioned.) By this point, police had changed the focus of their investigation. Previously, they were certain the true target was Genevieve Mulligan and perhaps her children. Now, they thought the poisoner was out to get the judge, though he wasn't home when the salmon was served.

Beleaguered servant Louis Mitchell was tried at the dawn of the New Year. On January 3, 1905, the jury was deadlocked. The retrial was scheduled for the middle of the year. James Mulligan Jr. was mysteriously missing and could not be called to testify. Why didn't the authorities subpoena him from Chicago? I don't know, but his conspicuous absence may have aided Mitchell. On June 28, the jury deliberated ten minutes and acquitted him. He happily said, "God bless all of you," and left with his wife. He never did explain the fanciful stories he told about a woman dressed like a man on the lawn and the masked stranger with a gun lurking in the kitchen. And if a

Mulligan relative really paid him to poison the lunch, the world never found out who it was. As the judge himself had written in his most celebrated poem, "Wrong is always wrongest in Kentucky."

Genevieve Mulligan heard the eternal footman snicker on June 21, 1915. The judge followed her into the hereafter on July 2, barely more than a week later. His children Kathleen, Marion, Dr. Louis, Alice and Willoughby were at the bedside. James Jr., by then an editor of a trade publication called *The Canner*, arrived from Chicago the next day. Mary Stevenson was living in Japan and could not attend the funeral. And that was that.

To conclude with an intriguing, heretofore unmentioned possible suspect: near the end of October 1904, Lexington Chief of Detectives J.W. Marshall asked police in Middlesboro, Kentucky, to help determine whether the arsenic used in the murder attempt had been purchased in that city. This was a clue unnoticed by contemporary papers. Of all Judge Mulligan's adult children, the only one who recently had been in Middlesboro was the newly married Mary Stevenson. Her husband was a military recruiter there. Did police secretly think she may have hired Louis Mitchell to be an assassin? Maybe they thought she was resentful because her father and brother James bitterly opposed her quick marriage? If so, police never admitted it publicly, perhaps because of lack of evidence—or perhaps they were intimidated by Mulligan's volcanic threat. In any case, there were no reports of a match between the drug in the salmon and the arsenic for sale in Middlesboro. Had they been the same, a sensation dwarfing all the others would have ensued, and today, Judge Mulligan would be famous for more than the poem that he himself came to detest. As far as choosing spouses goes, Mary must have known better than father and brother. She remained with Stevenson until his death in August 1921 and afterward never remarried.

22

THE WRONG COPYCAT

It was regarded as one of the most sensational crimes in Lexington history.

Around 11:00 a.m. on March 22, 1926, someone attacked Lewis (also spelled Louis) and Kate Hill, both White and age forty, in their home at 238 Rand Avenue. The weapon was a bloody hatchet that was left behind on the kitchen floor. (News stories usually called the weapon an axe, probably because that word sounds scarier and fits more neatly into a headline.) Their nine-year-old daughter, Lillian, found them unconscious around noon, Mr. Hill at the foot of the cellar stairs and Mrs. Hill in the front bedroom. Mrs. Hill was still alive but dying, her skull having been caved in from three blows. The papers reported that Mr. Hill had a fractured skull, but doctors thought he would survive.

Police had a theory about who their attacker was. Only a couple of months before, on January 19, the Clarence Bryant family, including two small children, were murdered at Cold Stream Farm, only four miles from the Hill residence. The assailant proved to be Edward Harris, a Black man, who was quickly convicted. He was executed on March 5. The police thought the Hill attacks were a copycat crime. They were correct, too—but not exactly.

Possibly acting on the assumption that if one Black man had recently attacked a White family, another might do the same, police arrested Percy Lewis, age thirty-three. To be fair, Lewis wasn't a completely unlikely suspect. He had spent four terms in the state reformatory at Frankfort several years before for obtaining money under false pretenses, horse stealing and escaping from a road gang. Lewis Hill had been a guard at the reformatory, and later,

Percy confirmed that they were acquainted. Perhaps Percy held a longstanding grudge against Lewis Hill. Not only that, but when the authorities took Percy to confront Mr. Hill at St. Joseph's Hospital, the wounded man positively identified him as the attacker. According to Hill, he had hired Percy to help repair a water heater. After Percy came to the house at 11:00 a.m. to start, Mr. Hill offered a secondhand suit and five bucks as payment. While they were at work, Percy, evidently insulted by his reward, stated out of the blue, "That's the way with you White people, always trying to keep us Negroes down." Then he struck Mr. Hill with the hatchet, and that was all Hill remembered until he woke up in a hospital bed.

Lewis Hill. *Louisville Courier-Journal*, April 9, 1926. *Courtesy of the* Louisville Courier-Journal.

In addition, Percy admitted he had been at the Hill residence on the morning of March 22, only fifteen minutes before the crime was discovered. He explained that he was employed at a tailor's shop, and his boss had sent him to collect payment from the Hills. He said he rang the doorbell three times and left when no one answered, unaware that the couple were lying unconscious in their house. He returned in the afternoon to try again, only to be greeted by a team of very interested detectives since the victims had been discovered during the interim.

When police searched his pockets, they found a knife, a new pair of socks and three jars of facial cream. The last seemed somewhat incongruous items for him to be carrying around, and it was theorized that Percy had stolen them from the Hills. A search of the house showed unfinished work on a water heater and tools scattered about, matching Hill's story.

It didn't look good for Percy Lewis, but he steadfastly maintained his innocence. He said that at 11:00 a.m. on the morning of the attack, and just before he tried to collect payment from the Hills, he was at home having a telephone conversation with E.D. Harrison, a coal deliveryman. He knew the time because the 11:00 a.m. whistle had sounded at the nearby Eastern State Hospital for the Insane.

On March 23, Mr. Hill had recovered enough to smoke cigarettes and discuss the attack, while Percy Lewis spent the day in a cell, fasting and praying for divine proof of his innocence. He said he had been framed by none other than Mr. Hill himself and prayed that Mrs. Hill might recover from her gruesome injuries, at least long enough to divulge who *really* hit her. But his prayer went unanswered, at least for the time being. After living fifty-three hours, to the amazement of her doctors, Kate Hill recovered consciousness long enough to whisper, "Oh God, oh God!" Then she died, just before 6:00 p.m. on March 24. The primary charges against Percy Lewis were changed to the murder of Kate Hill and the malicious assault of Lewis Hill. Percy continued praying, especially now that the witness who he claimed could prove his innocence was silenced forever. He said he would fast until "the Lord makes manifest my innocence."

Someone at the police department said, "Hey, why not test the hatchet handle for fingerprints? That might settle the matter quickly!" But by then, so many investigators had handled it that getting usable prints was hopeless. Dudley Veal at police headquarters expressed annoyance, stating that the attacker's identity might have been discerned had everyone kept their ungloved hands off the weapon.

Things got interesting at the coroner's inquest, held on April 2. Lewis Hill attended, though he was still recovering, and testified under oath that Percy Lewis was the culprit. Yet, despite having a surviving witness's statement on the record, the jury refused to name Lewis as the murderer, declaring only that Kate Hill came to her end at the "hands of an unknown party." They did not trust Hill's statement. He had been caught lying about when he received the money with which he supposedly paid Percy for helping fix the water heater. This was a small matter, perhaps. But what was harder to explain was that Hill's attending physician, Dr. Benjamin F. Van Meter, testified that his head wounds were "very slight," that he did not have a skull fracture as the press at first had reported and that he could easily have received the injuries falling down the cellar stairs, where he had been found knocked out. The doctor's professional opinion was that Hill had feigned unconsciousness.

As a side note, Mrs. Hill's assailant had wrapped a rug around her head. That fact probably didn't mean much to investigators in 1926, but modern FBI profilers note that in domestic homicide cases, the killer usually performs some "protective" act after the murder, such as wrapping the victim in a blanket or covering their face.

Lewis Hill must have been getting nervous by this point. If so, his anxiety grew apace on April 5, when the grand jury met. Carl King, attorney for the accused Percy Lewis, announced that he would soon have a "significant development" in the case. Percy would testify; indeed, he and his attorney were downright anxious that he do so. On April 6, the significant development was unveiled. Percy's alibi was proven true when coal deliverer E.D. Harrison confirmed that he had been talking with Lewis on the phone at the time the murder was committed. Roy Jones also testified that he delivered a load of coal to Percy Lewis a few minutes after the phone conversation and that Lewis was still at home when Jones left at 11:30 a.m. Mr. Hill, it will be remembered, said that Percy came to his house to do repair work at 11:00 a.m. and left half an hour later after committing a hatchet massacre. In fictional murder mysteries, clever killers figure out a way to seemingly be in two places at the same time, but in real life, this isn't so easy to accomplish. Since Lewis had maintained his whereabouts from the first day of the investigation, I don't know why the police didn't interview Harrison right away and save everyone a lot of trouble.

Kate Hill. *Louisville Courier-Journal*, April 9, 1926. *Courtesy of the* Louisville Courier-Journal.

The upshot was that on April 8, the widower was arrested at his mother's home in Nicholasville and taken to jail, protesting his innocence every step of the way: "I don't know anything about it. I didn't know I was even suspected." After the arrest, it was revealed that investigators had been increasingly suspicious of him for some time. Among other reasons, Mr. Hill had once before faked an injury for gain. Back on February 5, 1925, he claimed that robbers in Nicholasville had clouted him on the head and stolen $2,449 in cash he had just received from his father's estate. Bloodhounds could find no trace of these marauders, and Hill barely made any effort to have the theft investigated. It was widely believed that he pulled off a hoax so he could keep all the money for himself and cheat the other heirs.

What could have been his motive for killing his wife? Perhaps it was because Kate had refused to sign a deed conveying their property to an indemnity company that was suspicious about that missing money. In fact, had death not intervened, the Hills were scheduled to face a contempt of court charge. Kate may have been murdered because she insisted on doing the right thing.

The grand jury's probe into the hatchet slaying was the longest such investigation in Fayette County history at that time. Amazingly, although he had been arrested, Hill remained unindicted, and many thought he could never be convicted because Mrs. Hill had died without incriminating him. Also amazingly—or perhaps not, considering his race—Percy Lewis was kept in jail until April 12, just after Hill's official indictment. Lewis was certain that his petitions to the Almighty had been answered. Who can say for certain that they weren't? Soon after his release, he became an ordained minister in the Pentecostal Church of Holiness. The press noted that after Lewis's release, Mr. Hill was the only viable suspect for Mrs. Hill's murder.

To add to the many ironies of the story, Percy Lewis was arrested in July 1926 for shooting his own wife.

Lewis Hill did not confess. Nevertheless, it is all but certain that he was the killer. With the horrific Edward Harris–Bryant family murders fresh in everyone's mind, Hill probably thought he could find a perfect scapegoat in a Black man he knew had a criminal record because he worked at the prison where Lewis was kept. It seems too great a coincidence that Percy Lewis should arrive at the Hills' house to collect a bill so soon after Hill attacked his wife. It is likely that Hill knew Lewis would be dropping by before noon on March 22 and timed the assault to throw as much suspicion as possible on Lewis. Whom would everyone believe: a respected real estate agent or an ex-con? The story about hiring Lewis to help do a home repair and the scattered tools were all staging. As were the injuries to Hill's own head, which one might consider taking things a bit too far, but he needed wounds for verisimilitude. However, he didn't whack himself hard enough to make it convincing. Undoubtedly, Mr. Hill spent those fifty-three hours his wife survived after the attack in the greatest anxiety. What if she revived long enough to reveal the truth? Imagine his secret relief when she died, and how he had to summon all his histrionic skills to act the part of the grieving widower.

Hill's trial began on October 20, 1926. One thing can be said about him: he was tenacious, perhaps foolishly so. Although his accusation against Percy Lewis had been blown to atoms, he continued to blame Lewis. Perhaps, having selected his would-be patsy, Hill could not easily back down and now had to stick to his increasingly shaky story. Lewis was one of the chief witnesses against him in court. E.D. Harrison and Roy Jones once again confirmed that Lewis had been at home at the time of the murder. Hill's daughter, Lillie, testified that her parents had fought over property and that she had twice heard her father threaten her mother, once saying, "I ought to take a chair and kill you." Mr. Hill retold his tall tale about having been conked on the noggin and robbed back in 1925 but admitted he had waited an unreasonably long eight months to bring it to the cops' attention.

The jury retired on October 21 and reported that they could not reach a decision. They deliberated only slightly more than two hours, so perhaps they might have tried a little harder. Nevertheless, Hill would have to be tried again on November 15. When the time came, the trial had to be delayed again, until February 1927, because critical witness Dr. Van Meter was ill. In the meanwhile, Hill's mother paid his $5,000 bail, and on January 24, the accused stepped out of jail a free man. Whether he was permanently free or temporarily free, only the future would tell. But the smart money was on his "temporary" freedom.

The second trial began a year later, on February 14, 1928. Three days later, the second jury found Hill guilty with a recommendation of the death penalty. The prisoner looked as though he could not have cared less, but his mother fainted. Hill's attorneys demanded a new trial, because they had received an affidavit from a Lexington plumber named Stilwell who said he saw a Black man, not necessarily Percy Lewis, at the Hill residence at the time of the murder. In a separate affidavit, Percy Potter—there were more Percys in those days than there are now—swore he was acquainted with juror Charles Snell and that before the trial, Snell had expressed his opinion that Hill was guilty, and furthermore, he hoped he would get on the jury so he could help fry Hill's hide. This information raised the possibility of a tainted jury. In addition, defense attorney George R. Smith raised charges that jurors had been drunk when they convicted Hill and made a motion for a retrial. The twelve jurors hotly filed affidavits denying any such thing. It was turning into a war of affidavits.

On March 24, Judge Richard Stoll ruled that the alcohol charges were unfounded, excoriated Smith for bringing it up in the first place and even apologized to the jury for having their integrity insulted:

> *My experience with lawyers has always been that while they are and should be zealous in the defense of the rights of their clients, yet they do not file a motion in court, which necessarily must be prepared with due deliberation, attacking the characters of men who give up their time in the performance of a public duty, unless they are prepared to support their deliberate written statement with facts.*

But at the same time, Stoll ruled that Stilwell's statement was enough new evidence to warrant a new trial anyway.

Having won that victory, though not without public humiliation, on March 29, Hill's lawyers petitioned for a change of venue for the next trial

The Hills' daughter Lillian Hill. *Louisville Courier-Journal*, March 23, 1926. *Courtesy of the* Louisville Courier-Journal.

on the grounds that bad publicity made it impossible for him to get a fair trial in Fayette County. Judge Stoll mulled it over and then declared on June 9 that he felt Hill could get an impartial jury. Request denied! While he was in a denying mood, Stoll also ruled that Hill could not get out on bond.

The third trial ended with another hung jury. When the fourth trial rolled around in mid-February 1929, Judge Stoll again ruled against a change of venue, but he agreed that a jury could be brought in from Jefferson County. Proceedings had hardly started when, on February 20, the jury members were on their way back home. The defense objected that the trial should be set aside due to "incompetent evidence" being introduced when an attorney asked little Lillian Hill, by then about twelve years old, if her parents got along.

"Until the money was stolen," she replied.

A juror, who was not authorized to ask questions, butted in: "Where was the money stolen?"

Before anyone could prevent her from answering, Lillian said, "At Nicholasville." She must have referred to the robbery her father had faked in 1925.

The defense crowed that the jury member had broken the oath he took when he was sworn in. The prosecution and judge agreed, and the proceedings were over. No doubt, Mr. Hill was pleased with the anticlimactic ending to trial number four, but Judge Stoll again denied him bail, and on April 3, he again denied a change of venue. That took the wind out of Hill's high horse, if I may mix metaphors.

The fifth go-around began on April 9. A jury from Mason County was brought in. This time, we hear nothing of plumber Stilwell's affidavit that he had seen a Black prowler near the Hill residence at the time of the murder, so it was insufficient to convince a jury of reasonable doubt. Once again, the defendant's daughter, Lillian, appeared as a witness against him. Once again, Percy Lewis had to explain before a jury that he didn't do it.

The case went to the jury on the night of April 11. The verdict came the next morning. Hill's first trial ended with a hung jury; the jury at the second trial found Hill guilty and recommended the electric chair; the third jury was deadlocked; the fourth trial was declared a mistrial; and at the fifth and final trial, the jury found Hill guilty and recommended a life sentence. The only thing his attorneys could do—other than slip him a cake with a file in it—was appeal the decision and make a motion for *another* trial. His lawyer Smith vowed he would do exactly that. He did so on April 20, and Judge Stoll just as promptly refused the request, but he did allow an appeal.

Long story short: in January 1930, the court of appeals ruled against Hill. The sentence was affirmed on January 21. The press noted that the case made Fayette County's legal history for "the number of trials held for one offense [and] the number of jurymen called." Hill and his attorneys threw in the towel. On February 4, he returned to Frankfort Reformatory—not as a guard this time—supposedly for life.

But a "life term" often doesn't last a lifetime, either then or now. At some point, Lewis Hill got out of jail and spent the remainder of his days in Nicholasville as a handyman. On July 9, 1942, he fell off a building, fracturing his spine and pelvis. He was rushed to St. Joseph's Hospital in Lexington—the very place he had been taken to after braining his wife and himself with a hatchet. He died on July 22, 1942, and was buried in Nicholasville's Maple Grove Cemetery beside Kate, whom he had none too slyly murdered long ago.

BIBLIOGRAPHY

Overkill

Louisville Courier. "The City Council." November 9, 1846, 3.
———. "Correspondence of the Morning *Courier*." October 19, 1846, 3.
———. "Horrid Murder." November 4, 1847, 3.
———. "Innocent." November 12, 1847, 2.
———. "The Jury of Inquest." November 23, 1846, 2.
———. "The Latest Murder in Lexington." November 5, 1847, 2.
———. "The Lexington Murder." October 22, 1846, 3.
———. "The Mayor of Lexington Offers." November 8, 1847, 2.
———. "Suspected Murderer." November 11, 1847, 2.
———. "We Understand that the Body of Poor Hays." October 26, 1846, 3.

More on the Hazards of Shopkeeping

Louisville Courier. "Execution." June 4, 1849, 3.
———. "Henry and Aaron." April 16, 1849, 3.
———. "Murder." December 14, 1848, 1.
Louisville Journal. "Sentenced." April 30, 1849, 3.
———. "We Learn from the *Lexington Atlas*." January 31, 1849, 3.

Murder Among the Sweets, or: Jealous Much?

Louisville Courier. "The Execution of Weigart." August 14, 1854, 3.
———. "Execution of Weigart in Lexington." August 12, 1854, 3.

———. "Weigart Was the First White Person." August 17, 1854, 2.
Louisville Journal. "Bloody Affair in Lexington." January 2, 1854, 2.
———. "Fayette Circuit Court." June 19, 1854, 2.
———. "A Motion for a New Trial." June 26, 1854, 2.
———. "Weigart Sentenced." June 29, 1854, 3.

Frazer's Homecoming Surprise

Louisville Courier. "Acquitted." June 25, 1855, 1.
———. "A Correspondent at Lexington." February 17, 1855, 4.
———. "Disagreement of the Jury." February 24, 1855, 5.
———. "From Lexington." October 6, 1854, 3.
———. "From Lexington." October 10, 1854, 3.
———. "Horrible Murder Near Lexington." October 4, 1854, 3.
———. "The Murder." October 12, 1854, 2.
———. "The Murder Trial in Lexington." February 23, 1855, 4.
———. "Retributive Punishment." April 9, 1857, 2.
———. "The Trial of Gregg and Mrs. Frazer." February 15, 1855, 4.
———. "The Trial of Mrs. Frazer and Geo. Gregg." June 16, 1855, 4.
———. "True Bills Found." February 8, 1855, 4.

Darwinian Struggle for Life

Louisville Courier. "Another Homicide in Our City." February 18, 1858, 2.
———. "Convicted." August 31, 1858, 1.
———. "An Extra Session." June 14, 1860, 1.
———. "Fayette Circuit Court." July 18, 1859, 2.
———. "Homicide in Lexington, KY." February 16, 1858, 3.
———. "Letter from 'The Corporal.'" February 23, 1858, 1.
———. "On Saturday Last." August 19, 1858, 1.
———. "Reported Attempt at Poisoning." August 17, 1858, 2.
———. "Reversed." January 31, 1859, 2.
———. "The Trial of Darwin Payne." August 27, 1858, 2.

Lexington Lynching

Louisville Courier. "Letter from Lexington." July 15, 1858, 1.
———. "The Lexington Affair." July 12, 1858, 1.
———. "Terrible Murder in Lexington!" July 12, 1858, 2.

Hanging Some Dummies, or: The Tree Stooges

Louisville Courier. "Commonwealth vs. Shelby." "Shelby's Trial." April 20, 1848, 1.
———. "Correspondence of the *Morning Courier*." October 5, 1846, 2.
———. "Correspondence of the *Morning Courier*." October 9, 1846, 2.
———. "Correspondence of the *Morning Courier*." October 12, 1846, 2.
———. "Great Excitement in Lexington!!" July 16, 1846, 3.
———. "Homicide in Lexington." January 13, 1846, 3.
———. "The Jury in the Case of the *Commonwealth vs. Lafayette Shelby*." July 9, 1846, 3.
———. "The *Lexington Observer and Reporter* of Yesterday." July 23, 1846, 3.
———. "Shelby's Trial." April 3, 1848, 3.
———. "Shelby's Trial." April 10, 1848, 3.
———. "Shelby's Trial." April 28, 1848, 1.
———. "To the Public." July 24, 1846, 2.
———. "The Trial of Lafayette Shelby." July 11, 1846, 3.
———. "The Trial of Young Shelby." July 7, 1846, 3.
———. "We Hear of No Further Movements." July 20, 1846, 3.
———. "We Understand That the Trial." October 5, 1846, 2.

A Study in Calmness

Louisville Courier-Journal. "Bettie [*sic*] Shea Buried." April 4, 1889, 5.
———. "Betty Shea's Murder." April 5, 1889, 2.
———. "Betty Shea's Murderer." April 10, 1889, 2.
———. "The Day He Will Die." June 25, 1889, 5.
———. "Evidence Against O'Brien." June 18, 1889, 2.
———. "Gloomy for O'Brien." June 19, 1889, 6.
———. "Hanged at Noon." February 28, 1890, 5.
———. "Looks Bad for O'Brien." April 11, 1889, 5.
———. "The Murder of Betty Shea." May 28, 1889, 2.
———. "The Murder of Betty Shea." June 17, 1889, 3.
———. "O'Brien in Danger." April 6, 1889, 1.
———. "O'Brien Must Die." June 23, 1889, 4.
———. "O'Brien Must Hang." December 6, 1889, 3.
———. "O'Brien's Alibi." April 12, 1889, 1.
———. "O'Brien's Trial for Murder." June 22, 1889, 2.
———. "Poor Betty Shea." April 2, 1889, 5.

The Harris-Merritt Soap Opera

Louisville Courier-Journal. "Harris Acquitted." April 8, 1898, 4.
———. "Harris Released on Bond." December 25, 1897, 2.
———. "Harris Tells How and Why." July 16, 1897, 2.
———. "Indicted." December 17, 1897, 1.
———. "Jacob Harris' Trial." July 13, 1897, 1.
———. "Jealousy Still Alleged." July 11, 1897, 7.
———. "Judge Falconer's Decision." July 18, 1897, I, 10.
———. "Jury Gets Harris' Case." April 7, 1898, 5.
———. "Jury Refused to Indict." July 25, 1897, I, 3.
———. "Left Town." July 14, 1897, 3.
———. "The Right to Kill." July 22, 1897, 4.
———. "Woman in It." July 10, 1897, 1.

Wanted Alive, Not Dead

Lexington Herald. "Description of Newton Chenault Sent Broadcast." October 10, 1915, 20.
———. "Luther Hummins Killed." October 3, 1915, 5.
———. "Newt Chenault Evades Search." October 5, 1915, 5.
———. "Newt Chenault, Negro, Wanted Here." March 4, 1916, 6.
———. "Reward." October 12, 1915, 10.
Lexington Leader. "Refused Girl, Kills Her Father." October 2, 1915, 1.
Louisville Courier-Journal. "Governor Seeks Murderer." October 9, 1915, 3.
———. "No Reward for Slain Negro." March 4, 1916, 7.
———. "Was After a 'Rabbit.'" October 3, 1915, 10.

How to Scare Your Fiancée

Lexington Herald. "Furnishes Bond." March 13, 1930, 6.
———. "Girl, 16, Fatally Wounded." December 21, 1929, 1.
———. "Jury Charges Girl's Slayer with Perjury." February 26, 1930, 1.
———. "Jury Fails to Agree in Trial of Hatterick." April 24, 1930, 1.
Louisville Courier-Journal. "Bullet Victim's Funeral Today." December 22, 1929, I, 4.
———. "Fayette Jury Being Probed." February 8, 1930, 2.
———. "Fayette Youth Indicted Again." February 26, 1930, 11.
———. "Hatterick Hearing Set." December 24, 1929, 3.
———. "Hatterick Is Freed by Jury." February 5, 1930, 1.
———. "Killer of Girl Is Held to Jury." January 3, 1930, 3.
———. "Murder Jury to Face Quiz." February 11, 1930, 3.

———. "Negro's Slayer Moved to Jail." February 1, 1930, 4.
———. "Rites for Slain Girl Are Held." December 23, 1929, 3.
———. "Seven Prisoners Escape Jail." January 1, 1930, 1.
———. "Sister's Fiancé Kills Fayette Girl." December 21, 1929, 1.
———. "Weds Victim's Sister." February 27, 1930, 7.

A Hungry Horse, and What the Sausage Vendor Saw

Bourbon News (Paris, KY). "Tiny Mite Sold." September 11, 1908, 9.
Brooklyn Citizen. "Sentenced to Death for Double Murder." October 3, 1920, 8.
Brooklyn Daily Eagle. "Two Prisoners Freed to Face Murder Charge." July 21, 1920, 1.
Central New Jersey Home News (New Brunswick). "Woman's Tip Responsible for Solution." July 20, 1920, 1.
Hearn, Daniel Allen. *Legal Executions in New Jersey, 1691–1963.* McFarland, 2005.
Lexington Herald. "Greatest Offenders Against Society Dealt with Lightly." July 16, 1911, 23.
Lexington Leader. "Reward Renewed." April 6, 1911, 1.
Louisville Courier-Journal. "Deals Death with Tent Pin." August 17, 1908, 1.
———. "$500 Reward for Slayer of Diesbach [*sic*]." August 20, 1908, 3.
———. "Get New Clew [*sic*]." August 18, 1908, 5.
———. "Laid in Grave." August 21, 1908, 2.
———. "Sale of Tiny Mite." September 9, 1908, 5.
———. "Spieler for Murdered Showman Still Missing." August 19, 1908, 8.
———. "Tiny Mite." April 15, 1909, 10.

No Stopping Henry!

Louisville Courier. "Harry Daniel, Thirty Years Ago." June 30, 1855, 4.
Louisville Journal. "Henry Daniel." June 25, 1845, 3.
———. "Horrid Affair." March 8, 1845, 3.
———. "Melancholy." March 14, 1845, 2.
———. "Much As We Have Laughed." December 5, 1845, 2.
———. "Murder—Juries and Lawyers." July 1, 1845, 2.
———. "The Murder of Clifton H. Thomson." March 10, 1845, 2.
———. "The Trial of Harry Daniel." March 17, 1845, 2.
———. "The Trial of Harry Daniel." June 19, 1845, 3.
———. "The Trial of Henry Daniel." March 31, 1845, 3.
———. "We Have Received in Pamphlet Form." October 24, 1845, 2.

The Honeymoon Is Over

Louisville Courier. "Excitement at Lexington." July 9, 1851, 3.
———. "The Shooting Affair at Lexington." July 10, 1851, 3.
Louisville Journal. "The *Lexington Observer*." July 10, 1851, 3.

David's Bowie, or: Don't Fear the Repercussions

Louisville Courier. "At a Special Term." December 3, 1852, 3.
———. "The Case of the Commonwealth." August 9, 1852, 3.
———. "The *Lexington Statesman*." October 9, 1851, 2.
———. "Trial for Murder." September 13, 1852, 3.
———. "Twyman Acquitted." March 18, 1853, 3.
———. "We Copy the Following." October 6, 1851, 2.
———. "We Understand That the Trial." October 8, 1851, 3.

Fun at the Fair

Louisville Courier. "The Fayette Fair." September 13, 1854, 2.
———. "The Fayette Fair." September 14, 1854, 2.
———. "The Fayette Fair." September 16, 1854, 2.
———. "The Investigation of the Shooting Affair." September 21, 1854, 3.
———. "On the Way to Bourbon." September 27, 1854, 2.
———. "Outrageous Shooting and Bowie Knife Affray." September 15, 1854, 3.

An Entire Civil War Later

Louisville Courier. "Alexander Warren Rearrested." July 12, 1865, 1.
———. "Alex Warren Acquitted." November 29, 1866, 1.
———. "Attempted Suicide." August 5, 1859, 4.
———. "Change of Venue." June 25, 1860, 1.
———. "Letter from Lexington." June 16, 1859, 1.
———. "Lexington." November 26, 1865, 3.
———. "Lexington Races." May 30, 1859, 1.
———. "Mercer Circuit Court." December 15, 1865, 1.
———. "Murder in Lexington." May 30, 1859, 1.
———. "The Murder of Capt. Blincoe." June 2, 1859, 1.
———. "Stabbing Affair." May 28, 1859, 3.
———. "The Trial of Warren." December 5, 1865, 1.
Louisville Courier-Journal. "*Lexington Press*." August 31, 1875, 2.

Cheating the Hangman of His Fee

Louisville Courier-Journal. "Another Outrage." April 11, 1871, 3.
———. "John Bryant, Lately Confined." April 6, 1871, 2.
———. "John Bryant, Who Has Been." April 3, 1871, 2.
———. "John Bryant, Who Killed." April 29, 1870, 2.
———. "There Are at Present." February 6, 1871, 2.

Rashomon *in Kentucky, or: Choose Your Reality*

Louisville Courier-Journal. "The Circuit Court Convened." January 22, 1875, 1.
———. "Kentucky News." May 26, 1875, 2.
———. "Lexington." December 10, 1874, 1.
———. "Lexington." February 3, 1875, 3.
———. "Lexington." February 4, 1875, 1.
———. "Lexington." April 3, 1875, 1.
———. "Lexington, KY." September 29, 1873, 1.
———. "Lexington, KY." September 30, 1873, 1.
———. "Lexington, KY." October 6, 1873, 1.
———. "Lexington, KY." October 7, 1873, 1.
———. "Lexington, KY." February 11, 1874, 1.
———. "Lexington, KY." March 28, 1874, 1.
———. "Lexington, KY." April 1, 1874, 1.
———. "Lexington, KY." April 2, 1874, 1.
———. "Lexington, KY." April 18, 1874, 1.
———. "Lexington, KY." December 8, 1874, 1.
———. "Lexington Letter." January 31, 1874, 4.
———. "Lexington Letter." March 30, 1874, 3.
———. "Montgomery Parker's Trial." May 18, 1875, 1.
———. "Montgomery Parker, Who Killed." October 2, 1873, 2.
———. "The Parker Murder." April 3, 1874, 1.
———. "The Parker Murder Trial." March 31, 1874, 3.
———. "The Parker Tragedy." April 4, 1874, 1.
———. "The Parker Tragedy." April 6, 1874, 3.
———. "Stories of Revenge False." October 4, 1873, 1.
———. "The Trial of Parker." February 12, 1874, 1.
———. "The Willetts Killing." October 4, 1873, 1.

The Very Air Abounds in Kings

Louisville Courier-Journal. "After Money." June 24, 1912, 5.
———. "Big Jury List." July 4, 1912, 5.
———. "Bringing McNamara Back." February 10, 1911, 1.
———. "Came in a Bottle." February 13, 1911, 6.
———. "Claim the New York Man Not McNamara." February 8, 1911, 3.
———. "The Concealed Weapon Law." February 23, 1899, 4.
———. "Degraders of the Stage." February 13, 1911, 4.
———. "Dumb As to Movements After Kellar [*sic*] Killing." June 17, 1912, 1.
———. "Even Money Man Is Not McNamara." February 10, 1911, 1.
———. "Files Suit for Reward Money." March 8, 1914, I, 9.
———. "First Tip Came from Woman." June 16, 1912, I, 4.
———. "Five Years." July 13, 1912, 1.
———. "Frankfort Notes." August 3, 1912, 3.
———. "Free Man." February 26, 1911, I, 8.
———. "Goes After McNamara." February 7, 1911, 1.
———. "Has Offers to Go into Vaudeville." February 12, 1911, III, 1.
———. "Is Not McNamara." February 25, 1899, 5.
———. "Jury Secured." July 10, 1912, 7.
———. "Jury to Resume Deliberations This Morning." July 12, 1912, 1.
———. "Keller Growing Worse." February 13, 1899, 1.
———. "King McNamara Arrives at Frankfort Prison." July 25, 1912, 1.
———. "King McNamara Found." August 4, 1901, I, 6.
———. "King McNamara Granted Parole by Prison Board." December 12, 1914, 2.
———. "King McNamara in Tombs Police Court." February 7, 1911, 1.
———. "King McNamara Not Heard From." September 18, 1901, 8.
———. "Knocked Out Again." April 1, 1899, 2.
———. "Lexington Wants Him." March 1, 1899, 1.
———. "Magistrate McNamara." March 9, 1899, 1.
———. "Man-Chase of 13 Years Ended." June 15, 1912, 1.
———. "Man Held in New York Identified as McNamara." February 9, 1911, 1.
———. "May Be King McNamara." March 11, 1899, 2.
———. "May Be King McNamara." September 17, 1901, 3.
———. "McNamara Dies." March 12, 1914, 3.
———. "McNamara Fails to File Motion for New Trial." July 21, 1912, I, 4.
———. "McNamara Fined Again." March 31, 1899, 2.
———. "McNamara Found Guilty." July 14, 1912, II, 4.
———. "McNamara Has Final Sentence." July 23, 1912, 5.
———. "McNamara Is Still in Jail." January 10, 1900, 5.
———. "McNamara Ready for Trial." July 8, 1912, 3.

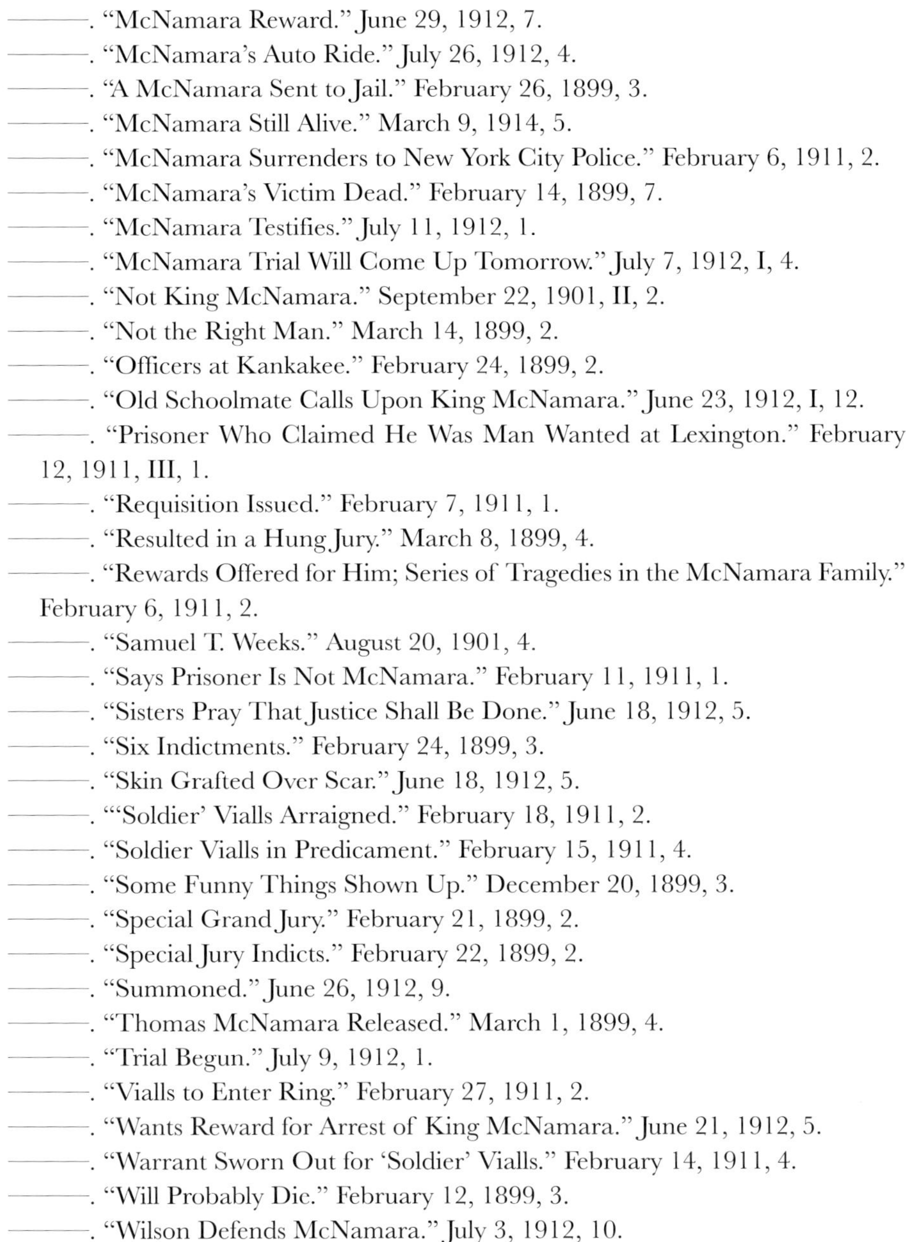

———. "McNamara Reward." June 29, 1912, 7.
———. "McNamara's Auto Ride." July 26, 1912, 4.
———. "A McNamara Sent to Jail." February 26, 1899, 3.
———. "McNamara Still Alive." March 9, 1914, 5.
———. "McNamara Surrenders to New York City Police." February 6, 1911, 2.
———. "McNamara's Victim Dead." February 14, 1899, 7.
———. "McNamara Testifies." July 11, 1912, 1.
———. "McNamara Trial Will Come Up Tomorrow." July 7, 1912, I, 4.
———. "Not King McNamara." September 22, 1901, II, 2.
———. "Not the Right Man." March 14, 1899, 2.
———. "Officers at Kankakee." February 24, 1899, 2.
———. "Old Schoolmate Calls Upon King McNamara." June 23, 1912, I, 12.
———. "Prisoner Who Claimed He Was Man Wanted at Lexington." February 12, 1911, III, 1.
———. "Requisition Issued." February 7, 1911, 1.
———. "Resulted in a Hung Jury." March 8, 1899, 4.
———. "Rewards Offered for Him; Series of Tragedies in the McNamara Family." February 6, 1911, 2.
———. "Samuel T. Weeks." August 20, 1901, 4.
———. "Says Prisoner Is Not McNamara." February 11, 1911, 1.
———. "Sisters Pray That Justice Shall Be Done." June 18, 1912, 5.
———. "Six Indictments." February 24, 1899, 3.
———. "Skin Grafted Over Scar." June 18, 1912, 5.
———. "'Soldier' Vialls Arraigned." February 18, 1911, 2.
———. "Soldier Vialls in Predicament." February 15, 1911, 4.
———. "Some Funny Things Shown Up." December 20, 1899, 3.
———. "Special Grand Jury." February 21, 1899, 2.
———. "Special Jury Indicts." February 22, 1899, 2.
———. "Summoned." June 26, 1912, 9.
———. "Thomas McNamara Released." March 1, 1899, 4.
———. "Trial Begun." July 9, 1912, 1.
———. "Vialls to Enter Ring." February 27, 1911, 2.
———. "Wants Reward for Arrest of King McNamara." June 21, 1912, 5.
———. "Warrant Sworn Out for 'Soldier' Vialls." February 14, 1911, 4.
———. "Will Probably Die." February 12, 1899, 3.
———. "Wilson Defends McNamara." July 3, 1912, 10.

Poet and Poisoner

Louisville Courier-Journal. "Answers to Questions." April 13, 1915, 4.
———. "Back to Regiment." October 24, 1904, 3.
———. "Case Against Lewis Mitchell." October 1, 1904, 4.
———. "Efforts Made to Find Where the Poison Was Purchased." October 27, 1904, 7.
———. "Exonerates James J. Mulligan." October 14, 1904, 2.
———. "Guards Placed Around the Home." September 29, 1904, 3.
———. "Held Over." October 9, 1904, I, 1.
———. "Indictment Against the Negro Mitchell." October 10, 1904, 2.
———. "James J. Mulligan." October 4, 1904, 1.
———. "Judge Mulligan Passes Away." July 2, 1915, 1.
———. "The Latest." October 8, 1904, 1.
———. "Limit Has Been Reached." October 12, 1904, 1.
———. "More Developments." September 30, 1904, 3.
———. "Mulligan Poisoning Case Goes to Trial." June 28, 1905, 3.
———. "Mystery in the Attempt at Poisoning." September 26, 1904, 1.
———. "Mystery of Attempted Poisoning Unchanged." September 28, 1904, 1.
———. "No Indictment." October 13, 1904, 6.
———. "Not Guilty Verdict." June 29, 1905, 1.
———. "Not His Best Production." July 7, 1915, 4.
———. "Passed in Circuit Court." December 9, 1904, 3.
———. "Poison in Large Quantities." September 25, 1904 , I, 2.
———. "Sensation Follows Sensation." October 11, 1904, 1.
———. "Strained Relations of the Mulligans." October 8, 1904, 1.
———. "Sworn Confession of Lewis Mitchell." September 27, 1904, 1.
———. "Unable to Agree Was Jury." January 4, 1905, 5.
Young-Brown, Fiona. *Wicked Lexington, Kentucky*. The History Press, 2011.

The Wrong Copycat

Louisville Courier-Journal. "Ax Murderer Is Held Unknown." April 3, 1926, 1.
———. "Ax Suspect Prays and Fasts." March 24, 1926, 1.
———. "Ax Victim Hit Thrice on Head." March 26, 1926, 1.
———. "Change of Venue Is Denied Lewis Hill." June 10, 1928, I, 9.
———. "Conviction of Hill Is Doubted." April 10, 1926, 3.
———. "Court Affirms Hill Sentence." January 22, 1930, 1.
———. "Fate of Lewis Hill Rests with Jury." April 12, 1929, 1.
———. "Fayette Man Gets Death Sentence as Wife Killer." February 18, 1928, 1.

———. "Fayette Murder Trial Continued." July 7, 1926, 4.
———. "Fayette Woman, Ax Victim, Dies." March 25, 1926, 1.
———. "Four Witnesses in Hill Case Heard." April 10, 1929, 14.
———. "Hill Again Is Denied Change of Venue." April 4, 1929, 4.
———. "Hill Denied Bail by Fayette Court." February 24, 1929, i, 3.
———. "Hill Denies He Murdered Wife." October 21, 1926, 4.
———. "Hill Gets Life at Fifth Trial." April 13, 1929, 1.
———. "Hill Indicted in Ax Slaying." April 13, 1926, 3.
———. "Hill Is Denied Bond." July 1, 1928, I, 8.
———. "Hill Jury Case Hearing Is Held." March 10, 1928, 1.
———. "Hill Jury from Here Dismissed." February 21, 1929, 9.
———. "Hill Lawyer Scored, Third Trial Given." March 25, 1928, I, 1.
———. "Hill, Lewis Heard by Grand Jury." April 7, 1926, 1.
———. "Hill Liberated on $5,000 Bond." January 25, 1927, 4.
———. "Hill to Go to Prison at Once." February 4, 1930, 3.
———. "Hill to Seek Another Trial." April 14, 1929, I, 4.
———. "Hill Trial Continued Again." November 16, 1926, 4.
———. "Hill Trial Is Set for November 15." October 24, 1926, I, 1.
———. "Husband Jailed in Ax Killing." April 9, 1926, 1.
———. "Jefferson Jury Will Try Hill." February 17, 1929, I, 8.
———. "Jury Trying Hill Is Discharged." October 22, 1926, 1.
———. "Lewis Called in Ax Death Probe." April 6, 1926, 1.
———. "Lewis on Stand in Hill Hearing." April 11, 1929, 3.
———. "New Affidavit Hits Juror in Hill Case." March 3, 1928, 9.
———. "New Trial for Hill Is Refused." April 21, 1929, I, 7.
———. "New Trial of Hill Sought by Affidavit." March 2, 1928, 1.
———. "Oral Argument in Hill Appeal Denied." January 9, 1930, 5.
———. "Two in Ax Murder Claim Innocence." April 11, 1926, I, 8.
———. "Venue Change Is Sought for Trial of Hill." March 30, 1928, 1.
———. "Woman, Ax Victim, Is Dying." March 23, 1926, 1.

ABOUT THE AUTHOR

Keven McQueen was born in Richmond, Kentucky, in 1967. He has degrees in English from Berea College and Eastern Kentucky University (EKU) and is a senior lecturer in composition and world literature at EKU. He has written twenty-four books on history, the supernatural, historical true crime and many strange topics, along with biographies, covering nearly every region of the United States. In addition, he has made many appearances on radio and television shows and podcasts. Look him up on Facebook or at www.kevenmcqueenstories.com.